On the Wings of
Dragonflies

On the Wings of Dragonflies

Reanne Singer

Words Abound
Ventura, CA

Words Abound
www.wordsabound.weebly.com

Copyright © 2017 Reanne Singer
Cover design by Reanne Singer
Front cover art © Reanne Singer

ISBN-10: 0692660917
ISBN-13: 978-0692660911

Printed in the United States of America

For Rebecca

In our hearts always - forever young

The second before the sun went out, we saw a wall of dark shadow come speeding at us. We no sooner saw it than it was upon us, like thunder.

...It was as if an enormous, loping God in the sky had reached down and slapped the earth's face.

Annie Dillard, Teaching a Stone to Talk:
Expeditions and Encounters

Foreword

Some losses cannot be healed but must be borne. To lose a child is an inexpressible sorrow, but still, words come rushing in to remember, to understand, to grieve, to scream. In this beautiful book, Reanne Singer brings alive the memory of her beloved Rebecca. Following a path paved with Rebecca's words, her own anguished and wise reflections, and quotations from many different sources, Reanne allows us to walk beside her as life unfolds in the wake of tragedy.

This book is built on the foundation of faith: the faith that memory matters, that Rebecca's legacy lives on, that she can become a part of our lives as she is a part of her mother's, and all those who knew and loved her. In some ways this book is a net to capture the essence of a person deeply mourned but also celebrated. Join Reanne on her wise, devastated, hopeful, loving journey and feel enriched.

Rabbi David Wolpe

On the Wings of

Dragonflies

One

How we spend our days is, of course, how we spend our lives.
Annie Dillard, The Writing Life

And so the nightmare begins...

I'm not sure what it was that we were supposed to learn from each other. I revisit the time we had together and capture glimpses of the last twenty-three years. Images float through my head, short frames of events that were played out years ago. I cling to these pictures. Your laughter, your voice, resonate in my mind. I'm determined to hold on to as much of you as I can. Don't fade away, I pray. Stay near; stay here with me so that I might reassure myself with these memories of you.

If I search my heart, I know you taught me to love with unrelenting fervor. Before you, I had never experienced such intensity, such unwavering loyalty and passion for another human being. From the very first moment I saw you, there was never any question that I would be willing to lay down my life for yours. How ironic that I sit here now, writing of our journey together without you still in this world.

People often talk about surviving the loss of a loved one.

Odd, that's what I am now, a survivor. How I wish things were different. How I wish that you were here and that I had not outlived you. This isn't what I bargained for. It's not what any parent bargains for. We are not supposed to outlive our children. But the undeniable truth is that tragedies happen and leave behind a wake of devastation. As much as I want to wish it away, the harsh reality remains—one of my children has died.

It's been three and a half weeks since your death, three-and-a-half weeks since I touched your arm or heard you tell me that you loved me. Can't we just go back twenty-five days and undo the horror? That's all I want—to make this stop, to pull myself out of this hideous nightmare that has catapulted me into a dark, interminable hell.

Three-and-a-half weeks, the words in my head repeat again and again—*and so the nightmare begins.* Your death is becoming more real now. I can't wish it away. Still, there are times when I believe that if I pray with all my might, you'll come home to me. I see you making your way up the walk to the front door. I hear your footsteps on the porch. My breath catches in my throat. With gaze riveted on the front door, I anticipate you crossing the threshold. Once inside, you're confused by all the commotion and wonder why everyone is so emotional. You apologize for being away for so long and not having called; you apologize for worrying me. But these images are all in my mind. They disappear and what remains is the reality of your death.

How is it that time moves forward without you? Winter is almost upon us, and it seems as though the entire world is preparing for the holidays. Hanukah is days away, and Aunt Leslie has asked me to go shopping with her. This is her attempt to nudge me back into the world. Baby steps meant to have me rejoin the living.

From my vantage point on the front porch, I see my sister drive up. My heart races as a young woman climbs out of the passenger seat of the Volvo. The long hair, the planes and angles of her face, create the illusion that it is you. I anxiously start to call for Bob to tell him that Leslie has found you, but I choke down the words as your cousin, Bria, turns and waves to me. The young girl is not you, after all. I swallow hard to push the pain further away. It lodges deep in my gut, a hollow ache that has become all too familiar.

My days are filled with pain. Seemingly innocuous activities lead me into dangerous territory. A walk to the park seems harmless enough until a young woman jogs towards me. Her gait and the sway of her body are graceful and full of ease. I smile, lured into believing that it is actually you instead who is approaching. When I realize the truth, I feel as though I've been sucker punched. You have died. Home again, I hurry to answer the telephone with the hope that it will be you on the other end. I need to hear your voice. I want to ask you where you've been. But you're not there. It's someone else. Time and again, I'm reminded that you are gone.

*   *   *   *   *

I am thankful for many things. I am most thankful for my life. I am grateful that I have a family with people who love and respect me. I am grateful that I am an independent thinker, with my own thoughts and ideas. I am also grateful that I am a Jew because I think we have some uniqueness and specialness.
Rebecca, 1996

Reanne with baby Becky

Two

Undo it, take it back, make every day the previous one until I am returned to the day before the one that made you gone. Or set me on an airplane traveling west, crossing the date line again and again, losing this day, then that, until the day of loss still lies ahead, and you are here instead of sorrow.
     Nessa Rapoport, A Woman's Book of Grieving

My mind flew to how dark it must have been…

It was Thanksgiving morning when the news of your death came. The day was clear and crisp, perfect weather for the holiday. The air smelled of fall. Up and down the street came the scent of roasting turkeys, pies and breads being baked for the upcoming feast. Bob and I took the dogs for a long walk and arrived home in good spirits. Our only task for the evening meal was to make a pumpkin pie. That left plenty of time for a late breakfast and a game of backgammon.

We weren't expecting anyone to come by, so I was surprised when Rocky and Zoey tore through the hall announcing that someone was at the front door. While Bob secured the dogs in the backyard, I went to answer the door. The clean-cut but very somber looking man asked me if this was your house. My mind raced. Were you in trouble? Had you been hurt? Maybe you were in the hospital.

I didn't say much except to confirm that you lived here. He asked if I was your mother and if someone else was at home with me. He explained that he was an officer but didn't specify what kind. He wasn't in uniform. The dress shirt and dark slacks seemed inconsistent with how he had identified himself.

By now, Bob was making his way toward me. I moved aside to let the man in. He motioned me to the living room and asked me to sit down as if he were the host and I the visitor. I remained in place and demanded to know where you were. He hesitated. My uneasiness turned to panic as I questioned if you were all right.

The man's face clouded with sadness. That was when I realized the awful truth.

His words floated in. "I'm sorry," he said. "There's been an accident."

I was cold, so very, very cold. My body quaked, and my knees buckled. I slid against the railing of the stairs and crumpled into a heap. The white banister spun in circles, gyrated above the caramel-colored wood floor. Bob and the man gripped my elbows and lifted me off the floor, then ushered me into the living room and lowered me onto the couch. I was suffocating, drowning. Everything closed in around me. I desperately needed air. I couldn't breathe. I had to escape. But where? I needed to hide, to protect myself from this man and his horrible words.

"Not Becca," I pleaded. "Please, not my girl." Someone was screaming. Was it me? "Not Becca. Please no, no…"

Your brother hurried downstairs and eased in next to me on the couch. The smell of sleep was still on him as he wrapped me in his arms. In a shell-shocked monotone, Bob told Jake what had happened. Your brother's bony shoulders pressed against me; his body trembled. The soft crook of his neck cushioned my tear-stained cheek. His face was warm and wet. When I drew back, I noticed how pale he was and so very sad.

The man told us that alcohol and the speed of the vehicle had played a part in the crash. He said Tommie had been driving and had been seriously injured. Two other boys also died in the accident. Another two survived with minor injuries. Tommie's was the only name of the five I recognized.

The assistant coroner apologized for not coming sooner. He estimated that the accident had been at one forty-five in the morning and explained that it had taken a long time for them to determine your identity. I know he was doing his best to reassure us when he said that you had died quickly. I struggled to take all of it in, but his words seemed garbled as though I were underwater and he was talking from somewhere up above. Everything was coming too fast. I wanted to tell him to stop, to give me a moment to breathe. But I couldn't get the words out.

He described the stretch of road where the accident had taken place, that two-lane ribbon that runs out past Temple from Ventura to Santa Paula. My mind flew to how dark it must have been. It's a rural road surrounded by ranches and orchards. There aren't any streetlights out there. It was chilly last night. Were you cold in that ravine? How long did it take before they bundled you up and brought you back to town?

It doesn't matter that he insists that you died quickly. That doesn't comfort me. I still worry about how you felt, how you dealt with the elements. Strange, the places my mind goes, the things I wonder about.

I stammered out a few words and asked whether your father had been notified. The coroner shook his head and told us that he didn't know anything about your dad living in a separate house. How could he? He asked if we'd like him to call your father. I told him yes, but then changed my mind, deciding that it would be better for your dad to come here instead. Bob went to make the call.

I don't know how much time went by before your father and stepmother arrived, but I remember thinking when they walked into the house that they had gotten there very quickly. Your father's expression was full of fear, his face colorless and waxy like a mannequin's. He didn't seem to know what had happened, but it was obvious that he was bracing for the worst. He later told me that when Bob had called and asked him to come to the house, he had worried that either Jake or you were dead. When he saw your brother sitting beside me, he realized that the news was about you. Your father and Cathy held on to one another, swaying as the officer told them about the crash.

As the news spread, family and friends drifted in. I huddled on the couch, most of me disappearing beneath a blanket. People swarmed around me, their faces mottled and red, their eyes tear-swollen. I know they spoke to me, but I can't recall the things they said. I'm not even sure who was there. I have a vague memory of people buzzing through the house, arms laden with food and flowers.

At one point, your father sat on the floor near me and stroked my head. "I'm sorry," he said. "She loved you."

I don't think I uttered a word. I just lay there crying and wishing I could extricate myself from this nightmare.

Somehow the day evaporated, and we were on to the next. Every day seemed exactly like the last. They are all the same now, all meshed into one hideous swirl.

*   *   *   *   *

When I was littler I used to like someone to read Good Night Moon *to me. I really like it a lot. I think it was my favorite because I really liked the moon and I also liked the little bunny that was going to sleep. I really was happy when I heard it. The thing is that when I was sad or mad if I heard it I would be very happy.*

Rebecca, October 15, 1991

Three

God is close to those whose hearts are broken.
    Psalm 34:18

Not to me, this isn't supposed to be happening to me...

The family stumbles through the first twenty-four hours, propping each other up, clinging to one another for strength. How can we be contemplating a funeral? This doesn't make any sense. How can I allow arrangements to be made for your burial? If we do this, if we bury you, then you won't be able to come home to me. And, damn it, Rebecca, I need you home right now! Do you hear me? Come home! The words rage in my head. Am I speaking them out loud? I don't know.

I curl into a ball and settle into a corner of the couch as if it is somehow safer there. I make my frame as tiny and compact as possible and disappear into a tumble of cushions and blankets. Deep-throated, primitive moans seem as though they come from someone else, *somewhere* else.

Two others have died with you. Two other families find themselves in the same hell as us. Somewhere in Ventura, two other mothers are crying, weighted down by this unbearable pain. They, too, must be bargaining, begging for things to be different. Like me, they only want their child home with them.

Three people survived the crash. Three sets of families must be overwhelmed with gratitude. How I wish that I, too, could chant their mantra: *It was almost my child. There but for the grace of God go I.*

Your cousins and your brother move through the house together as if there is some security in them staying glued to one other. Only occasionally does one of them break free to land in the arms of a parent, an aunt, an uncle. Later in the morning, I see Tahli perched in her mother's lap. Leslie strokes Tahli's head like she did when your cousin was small. It doesn't matter that Tahli is now seventeen and nearly grown. For this moment, she's a little girl full of sadness and grief, a little girl who needs her mother.

Grandma and Grandpa arrive. They look much older than they did the night before. The wrinkles on their faces are deeper and more pronounced. Your grandparents move slowly, deliberately; they seem so very fragile. Grandpa dabs at red, tear-swollen eyes. Who would have expected that your grandparents would have to endure such sadness? This can't be right; they shouldn't have to cope with the death of their first grandchild. But your death is now their burden. It is here for all of us to bear.

There are plans to be made, details to attend to. The coroner requires confirmation from someone in the family that it is really you who is at the morgue. Bob offers to identify your body. Where does he find the strength and courage? As I watch him leave, I pray that it won't be you he finds there in that cold, sterile room. *Somebody else, anyone else. Please, God.*

I want a reprieve. I want Bob to tell me this has been a hideous mistake, that you aren't dead. But he returns home gloomy and sorrowful, his expression a grim pronouncement that this nightmare is in fact real.

This isn't supposed to be happening to me! I want to scream the words, but they catch in my throat. *Doesn't anybody understand? Not to me, this isn't supposed to be happening to me.*

We plan the funeral. What a strange coming together for your father and me. All those years of conflict—the divorce, shared custody of you and your brother, and now we unite by arranging your burial.

Your father defers to me, promising that he'll go along with whatever I want. Some decisions are straightforward. Taking guidance from Jewish tradition, I conclude that you should be buried in a simple pine box. You'll be laid to rest in the Jewish part of the cemetery near Grandma's friend, Beverly. The details mount: there are pallbearers to choose, prayers to select, eulogies to write. I don't want to deal with any of this. *Please, God, don't let this be happening. Not now...not to Becca...not to us.*

Basic tasks become insurmountable. I have no appetite. Bob takes charge of feeding me. He plies me with bits of chicken, scrambled egg, anything he can cajole me into swallowing. Like a doting mother bird, he's now responsible for my nourishment. My skin and throat are dry and parched. I'm constantly thirsty. A stream of people keep replenishing my glass. They fill it with water, juice, iced tea.

I'm afraid to go to sleep, paralyzed by the very thought of it. I fight against it to the point of exhaustion. I am fearful of what I might dream, of what I will awaken to. I've already had the experience of forgetting that you have died. Sleep can work like a drug, erasing my memory of the crash, of you being taken from me. Sliding back into consciousness brings with it the cruel awareness of your death. That awful realization is almost as harsh and punishing as the first news of your demise. I brace myself and try to shield myself from the horror. Despite my struggle to hold on to consciousness, I eventually doze off. Sleep comes in small, abbreviated spurts. With each awakening, there is the predictable and harsh reality that you are gone.

One day gives way to the next. I'm amazed by the passage of time, astonished that the sun continues its cycle of rising and setting, then rising again. Your death has brought my life to a screeching standstill. It is incomprehensible that the world continues on as before. The days melt one into the other, each one indistinguishable from next until we reach the day of your funeral.

"It's almost time to go," Bob announces, his voice even and steady.

I hate the sight of his dark suit hanging on his bulk. I tell him that I'm not going with him. Doesn't he understand that this is too much to ask of me?

"You need to be at the service," he insists and urges me to change into the clothing I've laid out.

I eventually capitulate and don my black skirt and blouse. It is then that my hand drifts up to the hollow of my throat. Your necklace dangles around my neck. I reach for the charms, the tiny silver heart and the narrow toe ring you were wearing the night you died. These are my anchors; they connect me to you. These charms will allow me to walk out the door to the waiting car. They will help me make it to Temple and prevent me from shattering into a million pieces.

Bob navigates the windy road. How many times have I driven this with you and your brother? Each curve along the foothills reminds me of the life we shared. Bob heads out past Arroyo Verde Park, one of our favorite haunts when you were small. Another mile or so and we are at the turnoff to Aunt Leslie and Uncle Bruce's house. Rolling hills to the north, housing tracts to the south, and to the east...no, I can't think about that, can't face what is out there. I concentrate on my breathing—in and out, in and out. *Just keep breathing, that's all you have to do.* My hands are trembling; my face is wet. I stare out the window.

Breathing is harder now. I'm nauseated. "Stop," I tell Bob. "Stop the car!"

My throat constricts in a painful spasm. I gulp for air. He pulls on to the shoulder of the road. I throw open the door for more air. Bob's voice is soft, slow. He tells me to relax, assures me that he'll help me get through this. *One breath and then the next. In and out, in and out.*

He suggests that I close the car door, insists that we have to get to Temple. I acquiesce and sit in silence as he eases the car back on to the road. Another minute or so and he's turning into the parking lot. I want to bolt, run the other way. Doesn't he understand that I can't go inside? I can't do this!

He wraps an arm around me and steers me into the building. A few people are already milling about the lobby. I slip past them without saying a word, intent on a few private moments with you. Bob leaves me in the care of my mother and uncle, then walks into the sanctuary and clears the room of the few people who are there. Grandma Barbara and Uncle Sid are on either side of me, ushering me into the sanctuary. With their arms around me, it seems as though I could let my body go completely limp and still be propelled inside.

The pine box stands at the foot of the bimah. Grandma and Uncle Sid ease me forward. This may be the longest walk I've ever taken. *Breathe, just breathe. One step and then the next. Move one foot and then the other.* And then we are standing before your coffin.

I clutch your silver charms and rest my other hand on the smooth wood. Is it really possible that you are inside this box? The smooth, pale planks make me think about sun-bleached hay. You would like this color, Becca. It's the color of your hair in the summer.

"I love you, Becca," I choke out. "Stay close to me." I show you that I'm wearing your charms around my neck. I beg God to watch over you. Are my words meant to soothe you or me? Maybe both.

Bob comes up alongside and guides me to the Rabbi's office. The rest of the family joins us there, taking haven from the throngs of people who are now lining up outside the building. Planting myself on Rabbi Lisa's couch, I clutch soggy tissues in one hand and with the other hold on to Bob. The Rabbi's voice is soft and gentle, but I have no idea what she is saying.

From my vantage point, I watch the endless parade of people as they file by. The one-way glass provides me with welcome anonymity. Rising from the couch, I move to within inches of the window and stare in amazement at the stream of faces. Hundreds of people—friends, relatives, teachers from your high school, middle school, even your elementary and preschool. So many people have come to say goodbye. I imagine the silken threads in a spider web and the way they weave together, stretching out in all directions. It occurs to me that this is how your life is—so many threads reaching out to all these souls whom you touched when you were alive. These people have come to proclaim that your life was important, that you will be missed.

How I wish you could see this, Rebecca. How I wish that you could know that so many people are grieving. I want you to understand how deeply you were loved. I hope that you're looking down and watching all this from wherever you are. I hope that you're smiling at us.

The line moves forward, one person after the next slips into the building. Voices float in. There are stirrings as to whether there will be enough seats for everyone. Someone says that the sanctuary balcony has been opened to allow for more space. The rear doors that connect to the social hall have been opened as well with additional chairs set up to accommodate the throngs. Somebody else reports that one of the people who survived the crash is here at the funeral. I wonder who he is, what he looks like. Is he covered with telltale scrapes and bruises?

"It's time," Rabbi Lisa whispers.

She cradles my arm in her hand and leads me to the door.

I consider pulling away, but know that is futile. Everyone around me seems determined to go through with this.

I grab Bob's hand and trail behind our family into the sanctuary. An ocean of faces turns toward me. Somehow, I make it to the front of the sanctuary. I slide into a pew and reach for hands on either side of me. I suck in a deep breath and wait for the service to begin.

*   *   *   *   *

Maybe God communicates with me by encouraging me to ask questions and to be curious. As soon as I set foot in the sanctuary, especially if I am by myself, I feel God's presence. I gaze up at the ark and the star above. I feel safe here. I feel God's protection here. Sometimes it is overwhelming to think about God because of God's tremendous power.

Rebecca, May 16, 1996

Four

God makes me lie down in green pastures,
Leads me beside the still waters...
        Psalm 23:2

I look to the heavens, to somewhere outside myself, to know how to be,
what to do...

Your casket sits only a few feet away. I imagine you inside the box with eyes closed, hands folded across your abdomen. You are clothed in your favorite red flannel pajamas, oversized socks, and well-worn mukluks. I picture you swaddled in the patchwork afghan that I sent to the mortuary with Bob. He assures me that he told the people at the mortuary to wrap you in the blanket and then to drape your favorite sweater across you so that the bruises and scratches you sustained in the crash would be covered. I know, too, that one of your favorite stuffed teddy bears rests in your arms. I close my eyes and see the shards of ocean glass I sent for you. The shattered pieces of colored bottles have been tumbled around in the ocean and ground against the rocks until their sharp edges are only a memory. All that is left are the smooth, translucent surfaces— emerald green, red, amber, turquoise, ice. The violence of their creation has given way to time-worn beauty. The symbolism does not escape me. How I agonized about what items to have buried with you. Was there any way to know what you would want, what things would bring you comfort, bring *me* comfort?

The Rabbi's voice is strong and steady. I grab hold as though it's some sort of lifeline. Rabbi Lisa leads us through each stage of the service, insistent on us completing this terrible ordeal. I'm cold, shaking. I hold tight to your brother and Bob. Hebrew prayers wash over me; they mix together with eulogies and words of mourning. I look to the heavens, to somewhere outside myself, to know how to be, what to do.

Jake opts to have Rabbi Lisa read the eulogy he has written for you. Long after the service ends, I hear those words repeating in my mind. I am surprised by the depth of your brother's grief. How is it possible that until this moment, I did not fully understand the profound impact you had on his life?

Rabbi Lisa begins to read. "The last time I saw Becky was when the whole family was out to dinner on Wednesday night. She was doing napkin origami, and she was excited to show us how the napkin could be made into...let's say an object inappropriate for a restaurant. Most people would have been quiet about it if they had done it at all, but not Becky. She was running around the table, laughing loudly, and drawing attention to her accomplishment. This wasn't out of the ordinary for her; it's just how she was. What might have been lewd to the people at the neighboring table was simply good fun for Becky, a way to entertain herself and us as well. I remember her as a girl who loved to have fun and perform. She did her own thing, acting as if she didn't care what people thought, but deep down I know it affected her greatly.

"Becky had the ability to affect people, whether we liked it or not. She knew what buttons to push and how to leave a lasting impression. She was powerfully persuasive. She even convinced me, when we were growing up, to watch her favorite movies with her instead of cartoons. Because of her, I grew up on *Three Men and a Baby*, *Speed*, and *The River Wild*. I can't count the times when she would try to give me fashion advice or dress me up, and I would promise myself that I wouldn't listen to her, but ended up doing it anyway. She brought me into places where I never thought I'd be, and looking back, never would have been without her. That's part of what made her a great older sister, no matter how much I hated it growing up. I'm happy that in more recent years, we could view each other as friends instead of adversaries. When we grew up a little, I would truly look forward to experiencing her (not just seeing her) come into a room. Coming home from school was made sweet for me by the idea that I'd get to see my sister and talk to her on a level that was much different than when we were kids.

"I used to think about how our kids would play together when we were older, and we would tell them about how much we used to fight. I'd tell them how I broke her finger, but I'd also let them know that when we needed to be there to support each other; we didn't miss a beat. When we were going through our parents' divorce, Becky was my rock. I can only hope that she felt the support that I tried so hard to give her. I can't help but think about what more I could have given her. Another phone call from school, one more hug, a final 'I love you', or maybe an 'I'm lucky that you're my sister and I'm proud of you...we all are'. On Friday night, I was locking up the house and I almost left the porch light on for her one last time. Part of it was out of habit, because you never really knew when she'd be home. Part of me actually believed that she'd be back, and I'd get to see her in the morning, or maybe even that night if I stayed up late and waited long enough.

"In a way, I think Becky died the way she lived. She was stubborn, free-spirited, argumentative, devoted, loud, emotional, unpredictable, and beautiful. That's at least how I saw her, and I'm sorry to say that in her lifetime, she didn't see some of the good things that we all saw in her and still do. A pretty girl with a knockout smile, unconditionally lovable, a leader, a role model, a dedicated individual, and an integral part of a whole: a whole family, a whole community, and a whole world. I am, and I know we are all, less without her."

Rabbi Lisa sets aside Jake's typewritten page. I watch the paper float to the wood podium. I think of how snowflakes look as they fall to the ground and imagine how moved you would be to hear your brother's heartfelt tribute. The only sound in the sanctuary is that of people crying. My face is wet. Your brother leans into me; his frame shakes as he cries.

Other eulogies follow. Your cousin, Aaron, becomes the spokesperson for the rest of your cousins. He shares reminiscences about the seven of you growing up together in Ventura. Your father is the next to speak with Jake by his side, offering silent, tearful support. Once Dad is done, Uncle Bruce climbs the stairs to the bimah, each step slow and deliberate.

Uncle Bruce's voice is unsteady, his face washed out as he begins. "This is definitely the most difficult thing that any of us have ever had to go through and process. And to put into words the feelings and emotions that we have is a daunting task. Becca was a beautiful girl who had just grown into young womanhood and had her whole life waiting ahead of her.

"Almost twenty-three years ago, Becky came into our family. She was the most beautiful baby any of us had ever seen. We remember gazing at this awe-inspiring little child who could fill the room with wonder. She was curious about everything around her, finding fascination in something as simple as a yellow dandelion."

I shut my eyes and see you in those first days after we brought you home from the hospital, your face round with the tiniest, most perfect features that I had ever seen. When you were sleeping, your moon-sliver eyes perched above your dainty nose with a graceful up-sweep of a curve. Your small, feminine mouth was rose-pink against your soft skin. And when you woke, with dark eyes alert, it seemed to me as though you held the secrets of the universe in your young soul.

Bruce's voice draws me from my reverie. "Being the first grandchild in the family, Becca got some extra perks. There were frequent dinners with her grandparents and lots of field trips to the park and Santa Barbara Zoo. As the other children came into the family, they were of course included in these activities, but for the first two and a half years, Becca had her grandparents all to herself and they did whatever they could to indulge her.

"Becca's presence was always felt; from the time she was little it was easy to know what she was feeling. She could be intensely happy, bubbly, silly, and goofy. When she was upset about something, she let everyone know about it. As the oldest grandchild of eventually seven grandchildren, Becca was the one who choreographed the kids' activities. She not only directed them in dance routines, plays, and skits, she also decided which of the cousins were allowed to play in the games, and when. She created an environment of closeness between herself, her brother, and her cousins, having a special relationship with each of them in different ways."

What I wouldn't give for a chance to experience that joy again. I smile for a brief moment before choking on a sob. Why does Bruce have to keep referring to you in the past tense? I hate that, hate that everyone seems resigned to pressing on with this funeral. I squeeze your brother's hand and consider that if we both get up and dash out of here, we can stop all this craziness.

"One of Becky's favorite ideas of fun was to include her brother and youngest cousin in some of her plays," Bruce continues. "This entailed dressing Zach in her ballet costumes and painting Jake and Zach's nails, eventually leading them in a parade around the house or performing a skit. No matter what the activity of the day was, the other kids were more than willing to comply with her directives because they would do just about anything for her attention and for the chance to spend time with her.

"One of the things that Becca was most proud of was her accomplishment at becoming a *Bat Mitzvah*. Though it was a long, arduous process for her, the day of her *Bat Mitzvah* she was radiating joy and was absolutely pleased with herself. When asked how she felt about it, she said that she wanted to do it all over again, and given the chance, she would have.

"As you look around the sanctuary, you will see just how many lives Becca touched. She was loved not only by her family, but also by so many members of our community. One of the difficult things we have been dealing with is that it seems as if Becca is everywhere in this community. While having memories of her is a blessing, it is also difficult right now. As one of her cousins said, we don't want to have to remember her, we want her here with us."

I shiver as Bruce takes his seat. Am I cold or just spent? Mark Richman steps forward to talk about his remembrances of you as a young child. He shares how when you and his daughter were three years old, Aliza would refer to you as *Um-Becca*, a name that her family embraced for years after. I ease the tight grip I've had on Jake's hand and reconcile myself to sitting through the rest of the service.

Dr. Tom rises and tells us that he was the one to often see you at your worst, when you were ill and out of sorts. He talks about your appendectomy at age thirteen and the struggles you faced toward the end of adolescence and early adulthood when you tried to become someone in your own right, separate from the family. He mentions your strong spirit and stubborn nature. He ends with how much he's going to miss you.

I gather the tender remembrances as if they are fragile petals from some rare, exotic flower and wonder if it is possible for me to press these petals between the pages of a book to keep them safe. The words, the memories, these are what are left for me. They are the treasures I must preserve.

The Rabbi calls for us to rise for the Mourner's *Kaddish*. Though most who are Jewish recognize this as a central prayer for grieving. The prayer itself makes no mention of death or loss but rather is an affirmation of God. Nonetheless, that does nothing to ease me into the familiar lines.

I don't want to recite these words. They will only make your death all the more real. Bob holds me; his quiet strength surrounds me as the congregation begins the recitation.

"Yitgadal v'yit'kadash sh'mei raba."

A cry rises from deep inside of me; I hear myself moan and protest. My legs are weak; they feel as though they are going to buckle and I will fall to the floor in a pitiful heap of sorrow. It does not matter that I am not reciting the prayer. Today, your community has come together to say goodbye. There is no turning back.

The ride to the cemetery takes forever. The parade snakes through town. Once graveside, we are surrounded by so many people—a sea of sad faces swell across the well-manicured lawn. The pallbearers lift you from the hearse and carry you to the freshly dug grave. My throat tightens as they set you down next to the gaping hole. I'm dizzy and faint. Bob steadies me with one hand beneath my elbow and the other arm around me. My friend, Kevin, stands to my other side and braces me, buoys me up. I reach for his hand and clench it with such ferocity that I'm sure I must be hurting him. I focus on the rhythmic pattern of his breathing and hear my own heartbeat as it pounds against my chest.

Rabbi Lisa begins the graveside prayers. I gaze across the lawn and put names with faces. I want to tell these people to leave. If they would only go home, we could stop all this nonsense. We wouldn't have to bury you. But they don't hear my silent pleas.

The coffin is slowly lowered into the ground. I close my eyes and grab on more tightly to Kevin and Bob. The worst of it is the hideous grinding of the metal crank and the rubbing of the coffin against the earth. I need to get away. I can't bear the pain.

The grinding stops. No one speaks. Soft cries mix with the rustling of leaves in the nearby trees. It's time to throw dirt on your coffin. Bob steadies me as I struggle through the obligatory ritual that is viewed as a *mitzvah.* Judaism teaches that burying the dead is the final kindness that we can bestow on the deceased. How I detest the responsibility of seeing that you are decently buried. Instead of using the shovel, I grab up a handful of dirt. I want to feel the cold, frigid earth against my skin before I toss it on your grave. I want to take some of it with me, under my nails and smudged across the palms of my hands. There is no logic in this, only raw emotion.

The other mourners move forward to help bury you— Jacob, my father, my mother, friends, and community. Each shovel full of dirt lands with a heart-wrenching thud. The sound weighs on me.

Bob and I are the last to depart. I don't want to go; I am fearful about leaving you behind. I worry that you'll be scared, feel alone and abandoned. Bob promises that you're not here. He tells me that you are with God, on the Other Side. Still, I can't seem to shake the image of you out here all by yourself. What happens when night comes and it is dark? Shouldn't I stay and keep you safe? I can spend the rest of my life keeping vigil at your grave—anything to ease your pain, to ease mine. I imagine myself by your side, growing old here in the cemetery, waiting for death. After all, a mother should be with her child. I need to be here with you.

*   *   *   *   *

In the painting, Starry Night, I see a lot of stars and half a moon, and a big, long, black, scary tower, and a town and a church. Seeing this picture I feel sad and weird; it looks real still. I see colors like blue, white, yellow, cream, black, brown, light blue. I like it because it is quiet and calm and it looks like a good place to relax all day. In the night I would rather be somewhere else. I think I might get scared or something because it looks like a spooky place to be. I would be fine with an adult or a lot of other kids but I really don't like the picture very much!

Rebecca, January 9, 1992

Five

Give sorrow words; the grief that does not speak knits up the o-er wrought heart and bids it break.
William Shakespeare, Macbeth

Letting go was never easy for either one of us...

I've always hated goodbyes. Anticipating them leaves me anxious and weepy. The absurd part is that I can become emotional even if the goodbye has nothing to do with me. I cry at farewell scenes in movies, when reading a novel, and even when people whom I don't know say goodbye to one another at the airport.

Three years ago, you were preparing to leave home for college. As we packed away your belongings, I was struck by the fact that you had transformed from a child to a young woman. There was no pretending, no going backwards. You had grown up, and I could no longer make believe that you were going to remain with me forever. As you debated what to take with you and what to leave behind, I braced myself for the parting. Your going away to school meant that I wouldn't be able to see you every day. I would have to settle for daily phone calls and visits every couple of weeks. Now, that schedule would be a godsend.

When I showed you a poem that I had written, you became quiet. You were subdued as you read it to yourself. When you looked up at me, your eyes were filled with tears. Your hand shook as you reached out to hug me. The only words you said were, "Thanks, Mom. I love you." That was enough; it was all I needed. As you resumed your packing, I was left to wonder how I would ever make it through this next phase of our lives. What I wouldn't give for so simple a parting now.

Letting go was never easy for either one of us. When you were little, you had such a difficult time being away from me. Even going to sleep in your own bed was an issue. You much preferred sleeping with Dad and me. It seemed like an impossibility to get you to stay in your room. You were up throughout the night, leaving all of us weary and irritable. Oftentimes, your father and I would give in to you sleeping with us, simply because we were so exhausted. You would crawl in between us, and I would curl my body around yours and fall asleep to the rhythm of your breathing. When you were seven or eight, there were many nights when you slept in a sleeping bag on the floor next to our bed. Even that close proximity wasn't quite enough. You would call out during the night and every so often reach up to touch my hand to make sure I was there.

And then there was school. Your first attempts toward independence were tentative. You were eager to play with the other children and to explore all the activities at preschool, as long as I was nearby. But as soon as I tried to leave, you responded with heartfelt protests. I spent many mornings perched outside your class. I would fold my body into one of the tiny chairs and sit stiff and uncomfortable, while you played a few feet away. It was such a triumphant success when you were finally comfortable enough to let me leave for a few hours. I can't help but wonder if being adopted made separation more of a struggle for you.

Your voice is all around me. It fills the empty spaces in the house: *Mommy, are you there?*

"I'm right here," I tell you. "I'm right here."

I'm back in those early years, reliving all the *firsts*. I savor the moments of first words, first steps, first giggles. Infancy to toddler-hood, moment after moment of blessings. You were happy and playful, eager to learn and to explore the world. By the time Jake was born, we had moved from L.A up the coast to Ventura. Dad often worked late, which meant that once I got your brother down for the night, you and I would have our special time together. We read, talked, and recounted the good things from the day. Back then, *Goodnight Moon* was your favorite book. I read it aloud so many times that I knew the entirety of it by heart. You did as well, and if I missed a single word of the story, you would immediately correct me.

During that time, jewelry and clothing held a special fascination for you. Changing outfits multiple times throughout the day became the norm. You would take care to coordinate your clothes, then model the endless combinations you had created. Brightly-colored bracelets reached most of the way up your forearms. Remember when your favorite nursery school teacher dubbed you *Princess Many Bracelets*?

Five years old and it was time for kindergarten. You railed against that transition. Not liking the teacher didn't make the adjustment any easier. I can't say that I blame you. The Open Classroom, as it was called, was supposed to be creative and holistic. But the teacher was eccentric, with mood swings that put us all on edge.

The first day of school, I walked you to the classroom and stayed for a short time before departing. I was only part way across the schoolyard when you chased after me, insisting that you had no intention of remaining there on your own. Your face was flushed and tear-stained as you grabbed hold of me. What I remember most about that day was your thin frame jetting toward me, your long hair streaming out behind you. And I recall your slender legs poking out from your shorts and your knobby knees pressing up against me.

How long did that transition take? Weeks? Months? It seemed endless. I told myself that it was a new setting and that you would settle in, just like you had with preschool. And you did, but by the end of the year, Dad and I had concluded that the Open Classroom wasn't the best place for you. The year had been full of challenges. The teacher ignored the fact that we were Jewish and demanded that you join with the class in drawing a nativity scene. She would analyze your drawings of family, acting as though she were a trained psychologist with some special insight into your psyche. This was followed by barbed comments about our family's inadequacies.

The thought of you having the same teacher for the next two years made our decision much easier. We sought out something better and moved you to the Montessori School in Ojai. The oak-studded country setting with goats, chickens, and an array of dogs and cats helped you ease into the new school.

Childhood is, by definition, a series of transitions. But for you, Rebecca, separation was often the issue that underscored these changes. You were adamant about not spending the night away from home. There were attempts, of course, but you inevitably aborted those before the evening came to an end. You must have been eight or nine before you willingly stayed overnight at a friend's. Sleeping at Aunt Leslie and Uncle Bruce's house seemed to be the biggest hurdle. You explained that you were afraid I would leave you and never come back. Your reasoning was that if I ever decided to take off, I would turn your care over to Les and Bruce. But there was never any chance that I would abandon you. I was far too in love with you for that.

Mommy, are you there? The words echo in my mind.

Strange how I spent so many years helping you become independent, easing you into being able to say goodbye with the confidence that I would always come back for you; and now it is me who is left behind. It is me who rails against the separation. And I hate it, Rebecca! You dying, you going away, this God-awful distance between us—this is what we've been handed. I only hope that you're not having as difficult a time with this as I am. I would much prefer to believe that you have come to peace with where you are in your journey.

*   *   *   *   *

For Rebecca, With Love

When did you change from child to adult
did you wait for the quiet dark of night
was there a fleeting moment
when I glanced away
and you flew on gentle wings
shedding your child's innocence
for the woman you've now become

I can't remember
if there was a single point in time
when your face changed shape
when your brother's voice lowered an octave
I remember those transformations
as gradual, and oh, so subtle
like the coming in or the slow going out
of the ocean tide

But this...these most recent steps
have come so quickly
and I'm not sure I'm ready
no, I'm still waiting,
still holding on

So, tell me
when did you take flight
and leave your dolls and lullabies behind
when did you shed your child's innocence
for a journey all your own
         Reanne, Winter, 2000

*   *   *   *   *

Bio Poem

Rebecca
Short, happy, nice,
Sister of Jacob.
Lover of my teddy bear, my family, my dogs,
Who feels happy, important, good
Who needs love, food, water.
Who gives love, help, gifts.
Who fears night, Mars, shots, earthquakes.
Who would like to see a castle, a queen, a king.
Lives in Ventura, CA
Singer-Beilin
    Rebecca, 1988

Six

Take the herbs stacte, onycha, and galbanum — these herbs together with pure frankincense; let there be an equal part of each. Make into incense, a compound expertly blended, refined, pure, sacred. Beat some of it into powder, and put some before the Pact in the Tent of Meeting, where I will meet with you; it shall be most holy to you. But when you make this incense, you must not make any in the same proportions for yourselves; it shall be held by you sacred to the Lord.
Exodus 30:34-37

I would be happy to inhale the sweet perfume night and day just to have you here with us...

Yesterday, you were buried. Today, I stay close to home, moving about the house with a lethargy that is foreign and cumbersome. I am sluggish, unmotivated, tired, but unable to sleep. Bob and Jake roam the house, quiet and deep in their own thoughts. With eyes red and puffy, they wander in and sit with me for a while before easing away. Minutes later, they surface again.

Other people come and go — family, close friends. I hardly notice. They are a blur; their faces and voices drift in through the fog. I am numb to what goes on around me. Is that how I am surviving, suspended in that hollow space between life and death? Have I become so damaged, so wounded, that I've lost myself?

When evening descends, people arrive for prayers. This is the first of a week-long series of *shiva minyans*. Despite the cold autumn weather, the air in the house is warm and close. Too many people, too much talking, too many eyes that follow me from room to room. I don't even try to engage in the small talk, but simply accept the words of condolence with quiet resignation. Women from our Temple congregation take charge of the kitchen. They brew coffee and set out baked goods. An older congregant leads the evening prayers. He urges us forward in yet another phase of mourning.

At the rear of the family room is the couch you brought home with you when you returned from college. It doesn't fit; it stands awkwardly with its dark-patterned fabric in the already full space. But as I shrink into a corner on the couch next to Bob, I think that your couch may become a fixture here forever. I can't imagine ever parting with anything that has belonged to you.

The prayers conclude. Our guests rise. They edge into clusters, talk with hushed voices and shake their heads. Faces are held in taut, sad expressions. Jake speaks with one group and then another. I watch, then look away. When I shift my gaze back, he has disappeared. I scan the room and find him with another cluster. I think about the way a movie camera pans a scene, the actors drifting in and out of what is captured for the screen.

Leaving me in the hands of sympathetic friends, Bob circulates through the crowd, politely thanking people for coming. When he returns, it is to inform me that someone has been up in your room burning incense. He wonders if I have given anyone permission to be there.

"Only the cousins," I tell him, "but none of them would

have lit Becca's incense." I catch a whiff of the pungent scent. It smells like cinnamon and earth, like the rain-soaked eucalyptus trees.

We talk with Tahli and ask her if any of the kids have been upstairs. "No one wanted to go up there," she assures us. "It's just too sad to be in Becca's room right now."

Though I know most of the people who are here, there are a few new faces, friends of yours who have come to pay their respects. Bob suggests that perhaps one of them is responsible for lighting the incense. It seems far-fetched, but I am too tired, too full of sorrow to argue. Bob remains unsettled. He sees this burning of your incense as a violation. Someone has gone into your room uninvited, trespassed in the space that has become so much more than it once was. It is *your* room—the place in the house that holds the most emotion, the most heartache. And Bob's role as protector means that he has to remedy this affront. He goes off in search of an explanation. Perhaps this distraction gives him something concrete to do with his grief.

As I watch him go, I begin to wonder if the burning incense is some sort of sign. What if you're trying to make contact, trying to let me know that you're all right?

I spot my sister on the far side of the room and drag her off to the only quiet place I can find, the garage. When I tell Leslie about the incense, she suggests that you are here tonight. She tells me that she has sensed your presence.

Then she smiles and adds, "It would be like Becca to do this, you know, to light the incense so that you would smell it and think about her." She is right about that. This would be something you would do, Rebecca.

All those arguments you and I had over that incense! You loved to burn the sticks in your room. The odor was so strong; I pictured the smoke creeping out from under your door, floating across the hallway into my room. Over and over again, I asked you to take the incense outside or to keep one of your windows open and the door securely closed so that the incense would escape to the outdoors rather than permeate the entire house with its smell.

Perhaps the incense was a symbol of your independence. There are worse ways to set oneself apart, I suppose. In retrospect, the incense wasn't so bad. From my vantage point now, I would be happy to inhale the sweet perfume night and day just to have you here with us.

I am exhausted and drained from having so many people here. Aunt Allie offers to host the remainder of the *shiva minyans*. As the caretaker in the family, she is the one to rally in a crisis. Until this point, your death has left her at a loss of what to do with herself. Perhaps having the *minyan* in her home will let her return to that more comfortable role. And selfishly, it will be easier for me not to have so many people in our house. If Bob is correct about someone having been in your room, I want to protect myself from that happening again.

It is good to have the last of our guests leave. I consider talking with Jake about the incense and about Leslie and I believing that you were here tonight, but I abandon the idea. These things will only upset him and leave him more concerned about how I am coping with your death.

Jake kisses me goodnight before going to bed. Bob and I close up the house and head upstairs. We are silent, deep in our own thoughts. I am surrounded with the echo of your presence and whiffs of your sweet incense.

* * * * *

Jacqui

The tension was like radiation creeping from one person to the next. I couldn't see it but I could feel it all around me. As I walked by people I could feel their tension deep within them. People had tired, worn-out faces. The room was filled with cold, stark metal chairs that were placed in a semi-circle. The room was bare and somber. Facing the front of the chapel there was a worn, wooden podium and surrounding it were flowers of vivid pastels. The flowers were a vain attempt to gladden the room. Nobody said anything except for a few people making inane small talk in the corner by the white double doors. They were annoying; they pretended like nothing had happened, pattering on about the weather. The weather didn't matter. We were all here to mourn for the loss of Jacqui.

Hot tears escaped from my eyes as Jacqui's daughter rose to speak. It was painful to look at Anne because she was the last thing left of Jacqui. I grabbed for my cousin and buried my face in her shoulder as my mother walked toward the podium. It's ironic; I should have been comforting my cousin but here she was, my younger cousin comforting me. As my mom began to speak a knot formed in my throat like a steel anchor sinking to the bottom of the ocean. The words spoken became a slurred, jumbled mess. The only thing I could hear was the cracking of my mother's voice. Her voice knifed into me leaving me raw and open. I wasn't ready to let Jacqui go.

Rebecca, March 2, 1998

Seven

Memory is our defense against meaninglessness.
Rabbi David Wolpe, Making Loss Matter

Breathe, just breathe, I tell myself...

Eight days into mourning. Our first venture back into the world is to Temple for Friday night *Shabbat* services. Wanting to avoid the social pleasantries that typically precede services, we have made a point of arriving at the last minute. Even so, as I walk through the lobby, I am filled with the awkward self-consciousness of a teenager. Everyone here knows about your death. Their faces are full of compassion, but their expressions only intensify my discomfort.

As Bob leads me into the sanctuary, I find some brief solace in the press of his arm against my back. I take my seat alongside family. Images from your funeral rush over me. Will this sanctuary ever be a place of consolation or will it always be a reminder of your death?

Rabbi Lisa is already on the bimah. She looks at me and silently acknowledges my grief. The service begins, not with joy or reverence, but with sadness and pain. Every prayer cuts

40

deep, taking on new meaning, conjuring up bittersweet memories of the past. When the grief finally recedes a bit, the space is filled with pictures of you becoming a *Bat Mitzvah*. I see your thirteen-year-old frame standing at the lectern as you read Torah for the congregation. You were nervous, but also so proud and triumphant. What a day that was.

Thirteen! Remember the year leading up to your *Bat Mitzvah*? Your days were occupied with study and preparation. The biggest hurdle of all was you learning to chant. You could read the Hebrew, but the melodies were tricky and eluded your not-so-musical ear. Grandpa Mesh took you to one of your weekly sessions with Cantor Ralph and listened from the sidelines as the Cantor patiently sang a few phrases and then had you repeat after him. You gave it your best, but the tune you chanted was far different from his.

Grandpa told me later that you became frustrated and compared yourself to a friend who seemed to always chant without effort. Cantor Ralph did his best to reassure you. He reminded you that this was the preparation for *your Bat Mitzvah*, not for Samara's. He told you that you were creating your own melodies, bringing a part of yourself to the ancient tunes. Grandpa smiled as he recounted Cantor Ralph's kind words. No one but you cared that your chanting strayed from the traditional melodies. All of us were thrilled to listen to any rendition to which you gave voice.

The second biggest obstacle was finding the right dresses to carry you through the Friday night service, your *Bat Mitzvah* on Saturday, and the party that would follow on Saturday evening. The *Bat Mitzvah* was only days away. You and I had been to every store in town without finding a single outfit that pleased you. In desperation, I turned to Aunt Leslie for help. She hustled you off on a whirlwind shopping expedition. The two of you arrived home hours later with multiple dresses in hand. You modeled all of the possibilities for the extended family, finally settling on your favorites. I'm not sure who was more relieved, you or me.

When Friday came, the contingency of aunts, uncles, cousins, and grandparents escorted you to Temple for the pre-*Bat Mitzvah* service and festivities. It was well after ten o'clock when we finally returned home. Despite the late hour, you insisted on reviewing every prayer for the following day's service. My attempts to dissuade you were unsuccessful. You were determined. You and I perched at the top of the stairs where I listened to you recite every single line of the Hebrew text that you had learned. It was well after eleven when we tumbled into bed.

The next morning, we were up early—bathing, shampooing, curling your hair. Somehow, we made it to Temple for the photo session at nine. Then it was time. Family and friends poured into the sanctuary. You took your place on the bimah. Your face glowed with excitement. You soared, Rebecca. You did an incredible job chanting the prayers and offering insights on what it meant to you to be a Jew. You were the first of the cousins to reach this milestone and your grandparents couldn't have been more proud. None of us could. I was bursting—smiling, laughing, and crying with the pure joy of seeing the young woman you had become. That night, we partied, dancing and celebrating your achievement.

What a harsh, terrible contrast to where we are now. As I sit in the sanctuary and listen to the Rabbi lead the congregation through the prayers, I am struck by your absence. It hurts, a strong ache that overwhelms me. It seeps into my muscles and bones, saps the life and energy out of me. I want you here with us, Rebecca. I want to catch the sound of your voice as you chant the familiar prayers. I want to reach out and take your hand in mine. I want to smell the faint scent of incense still clinging to your skin and hair.

The service nears its close. Rabbi Lisa calls for those who are mourning to rise for the *Kaddish*. I pull myself to my feet and stammer out a few syllables before falling silent. I think how easily I could learn to hate this prayer.

I finally choke out the final words of *Kaddish*. "*O-seh sha-lom bi-m'ro-mav, hu ya-a-seh sha-lom a-lei-nu v'al kol Yis-ra-eil, v'im-ru: A-mein.*"

I can't get enough air inside me. The room is too warm, filled with too many people. I'm going to pass out, either that or throw up. *Breathe, just breathe,* I tell myself. My stomach spasms as I suck in a breath.

Someone leads the congregation in a closing song. Bob steers me through the ocean of people. He guides me out of the building and into the cold night air.

*   *   *   *   *

May you live to see your world fulfilled
May your destiny be for worlds still to come,
and may you trust in generations past and yet to be.
May your heart be filled with intuition
and your words be filled with insight.
May songs of praise ever be upon your tongue
and your vision be a straight path before you.
May your eyes shine with the light of holy words
and your face reflect the brightness of the heavens...
      Words from the Talmud read to you at your Bat Mitzvah

*   *   *   *   *

Over the long weekend I had lots of fun and adventures. Well, first I'll start on Friday night. I did a little part in the service because I'm having my Bat Mitzvah Saturday. It was really fun. I only made a few mistakes. Then on Saturday I was soooooooooooo nervous because I was going to do my Bat Mitzvah and I had to do it in front of a big group of people. It was really fun. After I got started I did great and then after the service on Saturday I had a really fun party and then on Sunday I had another really big party. It was sooooooooooo cool. And that night at 4:30 in the morning there was a very big earthquake. I was sooooo scared. I ran into my mom's room and we all got into the doorway and after all the shaking we all slept in her room and I was on the floor with my dogs and we were together. And on Monday we didn't have school so I stayed home and played with a friend and then I talked with some friends 3 way. That was pretty fun.

Rebecca, January 18, 1994

Eight

My sorrow is my castle, which lies like an eagle's nest high up on the mountain peaks among the clouds...
    Søren Kierkegaard, "Diapsalmata", Either/Or

I can't help but wonder why the world isn't shrouded in darkness...

The nights are long and I am restless, unable to sleep for any length of time. When sleep does come, there is still no break from the sadness. My dreams are filled with you. Perhaps the cruelest moments are in the early hours of morning, right before I awaken. For those few brief moments, when I'm in that twilight stage between sleep and wakefulness, I forget about your death and believe that you are sleeping peacefully across the hall in your bedroom. Then, as I slide into consciousness, the realization of your death descends with unremitting force. I am overcome with grief, as if learning of your death once again for the first time. The harsh reality forces the breath out of me, batters me.

It is not so long ago that I used to enjoy the beginning of the day with its limitless possibilities. Morning was a time of expectation, a time to anticipate everything good that could come. Now, all that has changed. Morning sunlight still pours through the window, but now it mocks me. I can't help but wonder why the world isn't shrouded in darkness. I am.

I plod forward, aware that others are keeping close watch on me. I think about my own death and imagine that it would not be so terrible to die right now. At least I would be with you, Becca. *No!* I scream the word loud inside my head and summon forth every bit of resolve to push away the thought of dying. I cannot allow myself to give in to the idea of death. Jake needs me.

Your brother has returned up north to finish out the semester at U.C. Davis. His departure leaves me with more loss and loneliness. If only I were reassured by the fact that he will be home again in a few weeks. But this will only be a short reprieve. He will be home for a month before leaving for a year-long study abroad program in Australia. I desperately want him to stay close to home but refuse to ask that of him. Jake's life has to be more than taking care of me.

With him back at school and Bob at work, I have too much time alone. There is too much opportunity for introspection, too much time to rattle around this quiet, empty house.

Condolence cards arrive daily. I sift through the envelopes and write endless thank-you notes to those who have made contributions to various charities. I read the words that people have scrawled on the inside of the cards, then band the cards into sturdy bundles and pack them safely into a box that I store in your closet. I could toss out these cards. Is there really any reason to hang on to them? But they contain prayers for healing and memories of you. I have to keep these remnants safe, keep you safe.

I undo a bundle and open one of the cards again to read the words that are printed against the background of a star-studded sky:

Perhaps they are not the stars,
But rather openings in heaven
Where the love of our lost ones
Pours through
And shines upon us
To let us know they are happy.

There is no author, only the citation at the bottom: *Inspired by an Eskimo legend.* The poem remains with me long after I leave your room.

Late that night, I walk out to the front yard and stare at the winter sky. Shimmering stars float in the velvet darkness. Is one of these stars you, Bec? The hope soothes me. It is odd where I find comfort these days.

The following day, another card arrives from the mother of one of your friends. The handwritten inscription is full of kind words that make me feel less alone: *This tragedy could have happened in any of our families, to any of our children.* These words erase some of the stigma that has accompanied your death. Your friend's mother helps me believe that your death is not some harsh punishment for me being an imperfect mother or you an imperfect child. Our family has not been singled out. We are simply the unfortunate survivors of a terrible, terrible tragedy.

A second condolence card brings with it the gift of pictures from an earlier time. You must have been about eight or nine when the photos were taken. You are posing with two friends, the three of you donning sunglasses and smiling in big, toothy grins, the kind that kids have before they've completely grown into their permanent teeth. The picture was taken at a birthday celebration for your friend, Meredith. All of you had been asked to dress in 1950's attire. You had so much fun that day. Life was simpler then, safer, or so it seems to me.

*   *   *   *   *

Emily and Meredith were best friends who had the luxury of living right across the street from one another. They willingly included you in their escapades, but you wanted more than that. You wanted to be as important to each of them as they were to each other. Emily and Meredith—their names were usually spoken back to back. The two girls seemed inseparable. That's why it was out of the ordinary that on this particular day only Emily came to visit.

Though the same age, Emily towered inches above you. There was an ease to your conversation and play. The two of you were never at a loss for things to do. Riding bikes, roller skating, swimming, dancing—the two of you enjoyed it all.

On this particular day, you and Emily were upstairs, making your objections known about Jake wanting to be included. The sounds shifted to peals of laughter followed by Emily's angry shrieks. Footsteps pounded down to the kitchen. Emily was the first to appear.

"He threw my shoe in the toilet," she announced. Emily was clearly upset. "Jake took my shoe, and it's in the toilet!"

You and your brother fell in a few steps behind her.

"She was teasing me," Jake explained.

You remained quiet, choosing not to side with either one. I stifled a smile and followed the three of you upstairs to assess the damage. Sure enough, Emily's tennis shoe was submerged underwater.

"I'm sure it will be all right," I offered, but Emily refused to be so easily calmed.

I pulled the shoe from the toilet and had six-year-old Jake help me clean it. He returned the soggy shoe to Emily with an apology.

That became the infamous *Emily Story*. Years later, Emily would continue to remind your brother about that infraction. It became a part of the history the three of you shared.

So many stories for too short a lifetime. I am terrified that I might forget them. Writing them down reassures me and helps ease the fear. I journal, doing my best to preserve everything I can about you and the time we had together. My writing offers me sanity; it gives me something concrete to grab hold of. I don't know if I'll ever share these ramblings with others. The writing, the remembering, is what I crave. It is what is important to me. Putting our memories down on paper makes them more real, more tangible. I think you would like it that I'm writing all this down. I think you would want me to understand who you were and to remember.

*   *   *   *   *

I remember when I was younger and all my friends knew how to ride a bike. I kept trying but every time I tried to get on the bike I would immediately fall right off. This started to really bother me because all my friends that lived in my neighborhood would all go on their bikes and I felt really left out because I couldn't ride a bike. One Saturday morning I decided to go outside when nobody was out there and I got on the bike even though it was scary and I was worried that I would fall off again. When I got on the bike, to my surprise, instead of falling off I rode all the way from my house to the corner. I was so proud.

Rebecca, April 6, 1995

Becky at 6 with Jake

Nine

Surely there is a God in this place and I did not know it.
Genesis 28:1-19

A parent shouldn't have to bury a child, shouldn't have to mourn for a life cut short...

Most young people take the gift of life for granted. I know that, but the realization does nothing to console me. It doesn't change the fact that you were one of those kids who saw yourself as invincible and immortal. It doesn't bring you back.

The risks you took scared me. I hated the late hours you kept. I worried that you were smoking, fretted about the long drives you so loved to take, was concerned about where you were, the friends you were with. You tried to reassure me, told me that everything would be fine. But it's not fine, Rebecca! You've been gone for a month now, and I can't help but wonder if things would have turned out differently if I'd insisted on you making better choices. I am left to question whether I would still have you here with me if only you had been more careful, if only I had warned you one more time about the dangers out there. If I had only begged you not to leave the house that night.

Over and over again, I think about that evening. I run through each segment of time. I pour over the sequence of events as if there is some sense to be made of all this. If I understand it, analyze it in just the right way, then maybe I will be able to change what has happened.

I picture you at the front door, purse in hand, overnight bag slung over your shoulder.

"Will you be home tonight?" I ask.

"I don't know, Mom," you tell me. "I might stay at Stacey's."

"I'm uncomfortable when I don't know whether or not to expect you home," I say. "I worry about you, Becca."

You sigh. Is that exasperation or empathy? I'm not sure.

"I know, Mom," you respond. "But you worry too much. Everything's fine. Really it is." Your shrug is careless, casual.

You see me as overprotective, believe that I treat you as though you're younger and less capable than you really are. This doesn't stop me from saying more.

"I don't want you to get hurt or..." My voice trails off at the thought of the potential dangers.

"I'm sorry," you say. "I'm sorry that the way I live scares you. I take care of myself, Mom. Honest."

Right, I think. *At twenty-two years old, how can you take care of yourself?* But I don't say that. Instead, I ask if I should leave the porch light on for you.

Another shrug of your shoulders. You don't have an answer for me.

"I hate to leave it on all night if you aren't coming home," I continue, halfway believing that by saying this, I'll convince you to make it an early evening.

"Then don't leave the light on." Your tone is dismissive. You tag on a jab. "I just hope nothing happens to me later on when I'm going from the car to the house."

The barbed comment has had its desired effect. It has left me feeling guilty and afraid. Both of us are taken aback by the weight of your words.

You are quick to offer a conciliatory smile. You reach out a hand. "I'm sorry. I didn't mean it. I'll be fine. Don't worry about leaving the light on all night." You offer a hug and then are out the door, tossing an *I love you* over your shoulder.

"I love you, too." I watch you climb into your car and drive away.

The next day, after the coroner's assistant has told us that you have died, I revisit the events of that night. How I wish that I had held on tight and told you that I didn't want you to leave. There would have been an argument, but I could have insisted that you stay home. Perhaps then, you would be safe. I would have the rest of my life to spend with you.

That's the way it's supposed to be, you know. A parent is supposed to have her children forever. I was supposed to nurture and protect you, watch you move through adulthood. I was going to dance at your wedding, buy you maternity clothes when you were pregnant, help you decorate the baby's room. I was going to be there when you gave birth. When I grew old, you would be nearby and see me through that phase of my life. You used to tell me that if I needed to, I could live with you when I was old. You were quick to add that you would be in charge, though, not me.

A parent shouldn't have to bury a child, shouldn't have to mourn for a life cut short. A parent shouldn't have to learn how to go on living after such a loss. But that is exactly what I am doing—struggling to make sense out of life, fighting to make it from one day to the next, reaching for the strength not to become one of those people who walks around with a huge, gaping hole in her heart for all to see.

I used to believe that the worst thing a parent could face would be the death of her child. I no longer think that. The coroner has concluded that your neck was most likely broken at the time of impact. Chances are that had you survived, you would have been paralyzed for life. You would have detested that. It truly would have been a fate worse than death. I would much rather go through the rest of my life missing you than having you endure such torment.

In the first days after your death, I could not comprehend how God could allow this to happen. What kind of God wrenches a twenty-two year old from life and leaves her parents and family behind to grieve?

When a friend from Temple came to visit, we talked about this. Deborah asked me where God was in the Holocaust. She shook her head. "God wasn't there when millions of people were killed in the camps, God wasn't there when Becky was killed. Her death was a terrible accident, but God wasn't there. God didn't have a hand in this."

Deborah's words allow me to have faith in a Higher Spirit. If I believed that God had caused your death, I wouldn't want anything to do with such a God. My God gives us free will, gives us rational minds and the ability to know right from wrong. God gives us the capacity to love. God doesn't move us about like inanimate pieces in a chess game. We are given the power to weigh decisions, to make choices, and to understand the consequences of our behaviour.

The problem is that even if we lead righteous lives, even if we move through our days so that we are accountable to ourselves and to those around us, there is no guarantee that we will escape misfortune and tragedy.

Years ago, I had the privilege of hearing Rabbi Harold Kushner speak about this within the context of the death of his young son. At the time, his words impressed me. Now, they are far more profound than ever.

Without this book, his (Aaron's) death would have been just a statistic, a private tragedy. But I believe that God, who did not send the illness and could not prevent it, did for me what He does for so

many grieving people. He gave me the strength and the wisdom to take my personal sorrow and forge it into an instrument of redemption, which would help others. As in Samson's riddle in the Book of Judges (14:14), "Out of the fierce came something sweet, and out of death, the sustaining of life."
  Rabbi Harold Kushner

Your death has motivated me to once again read his book, *When Bad Things Happen to Good People.* Like Rabbi Kushner, I am surviving the loss of a child. Like him, I have to find meaning and strength in what remains of my life.

* * * * *

Life is too precious and if you have goals you want to achieve then you better start working towards them because you never know what might happen. There are so many goals I have and things I want to do and see before I die so I better start now because I never know when I might die. Life is precious because there is so much you can do with time. It is good to fill each day with meaning and it is not good to waste time. I am still learning how to do this and I am working very hard at it.
  Rebecca, April 3, 1995

Ten

Nothing is an adequate substitute for presence. And death steals presence. For that alone, it is difficult for us to forgive the design of this world.

Rabbi David Wolpe, Making Loss Matter

Tears come at such unexpected times...

Jake is home from school. We will have him here for one month before he leaves for Australia. As I walk into his room, I find him perched in front of his laptop. Sprawled across the screen is a large picture of you putting makeup on your cousin, Bria. Your expression is solemn and intent, hers one of complete trust.

I am surprised by the picture and the fact that your brother has chosen to have this as his screen-saver. I swallow against the lump in my throat before asking him to print out a copy for me. Why is it so important for me to shield him from my emotions? Jake needs to see me cry, needs permission to cry himself. I push on and ask if he has more photos of you. When he promises to look, I shove down a sob and escape to the privacy of the bathroom. When I look in the mirror, a tired, withered face stares back at me and then crumples in sorrow.

*   *   *   *   *

Weekends when you and Jake were growing up were often filled with family get-togethers. Given your passion for dance and theater, you frequently chose to choreograph the other children in productions. This night was no exception.

Mariah Carey's voice floated in from the living room where the seven of you were busy rehearsing. Rehearsals continued until the performance met with your approval. The troops didn't grumble or complain. They were happy to yield to your wishes, eager to please and to be included.

Every once in awhile, a cousin would wander through the kitchen on their way to the family room where we stored the dress-up clothes. Coming back through the kitchen, your cousins' arms would be overflowing with colorful skirts, scarves, and vests—a rainbow assortment to add to the theatrical endeavor.

Dinner signaled a break in the practice sessions. Noise flooded the room as family filled their plates with food and then caught up on the activities of the past week. Once the meal was over and dishes washed, it was time for the show. You announced the night's entertainment and turned on the music, then dashed out of sight to the adjoining hallway. Seconds later you made your dramatic entrance. Your brother and five cousins were not far behind, young ducklings that had imprinted on their mother. Proud, expectant smiles and giggles from the brood accompanied their march in to Mariah Carey's *Hero.* You had the cousins doing moves from ballet and modern dance. A quick change of costume and the music switched to the theme from *Chorus Line.*

The seven of you danced with varying degrees of gracefulness, but the adults were happy to watch the show. At the end of the routine, your audience broke into resounding applause while you and your cousins took your bows.

* * * * *

Tears come at such unexpected times. I manage to burn myself while pulling a pan of chicken from the oven, something your brother and you would have found predictable. As I submerge my hand into a bowl of ice water, old photos of you and Jake on the side of the refrigerator catch my attention. The pictures were taken years ago during a trip to the L.A. Zoo. You were about six, your brother four. Your face was painted like a clown; your broad smile attested to how much fun we had that day. My tears return; not soft, gentle ones, but harsh tears that cause my throat and gut to constrict. I miss you so much, Becca. Your absence leaves me doubled over and gasping for air.

Bob turns on the television. I sit with him as he watches a basketball game. One of the players dashes across the court. I notice his petite, perfectly formed ears and find myself crying all over again. When Bob asks what's wrong, I sputter out something about the man's ears reminding me of yours. Bob strokes my forehead until my crying stops.

It is pointless to brace myself against the grief. It comes in waves, ebbing and receding like the ocean currents, sometimes sneaking in with such incredible stealth that I fail to notice until it is right on top of me. Fighting against the sadness is far more exhausting than giving in to it. It is easier to ride the waves and allow the grief to take me where it will rather than railing against it. I can survive it. This is a new awareness.

My grief has not eased. If anything, it seems stronger than it was in the beginning. You are in my thoughts all the time. Waking, sleeping, dreaming; it doesn't matter what I am doing. You are right here with me. Your presence surrounds me and mixes with the pain of not having you in this world.

*   *   *   *   *

My Personality Collage

For my personality collage, I chose things that represent me. There are many things I like to do and enjoy. Some are very different from one another. Some of the things which I most enjoy are sunflowers, music, traveling, taking pictures, writing, the beach, and most of all, dancing.

I'm really not sure why I like sunflowers, but I think that they are really neat to look at. They are big and bright. I also like to eat the dried seeds. I like to watch the flowers wave in the wind.

I have included a CD tape player which is what I have. I listen to music almost all the time. I love to choreograph dances of my own or dance one that a teacher or friend has made up with me. I can choreograph a dance to just about any music or song by listening to the beat.

I selected a map which represents traveling. I love to travel but I don't get to go on very many vacations except in the summer. I have been to many places but I really love to go camping which is my favorite. It is fun to go hiking and swimming in the creek. I also love to share a tent with my friends.

I put a camera on my paper because no matter where I am, I love to take pictures of family, friends, animals, and lots more. I think pictures are very important because they help you to remember the past. That time may never happen again because you can't repeat the past.

I included a picture of writing tools like pens and pencils and other things because I love to write. One of my favorite things I really enjoy doing is exchanging letters with friends. I love to write letters, but it is much more fun receiving them. It keeps one in touch with my friends that have moved far away.

I love the beach! I go to the beach almost all of the time in the summer because my grandparents have a house on the beach here in Ventura. I can remember so many good times I have had there. I remember making sandcastles with friends or cousins, taking a run to the pier with a friend, digging for sand crabs with my brother, and just having fun in the water.

Dance. Dancing is my life in another way. If I could dance every day, I would. It is a way to express myself, a way to be with friends, and a way to challenge myself physically. There is always more to learn by watching and doing. I spend hours and hours dancing a week, but I also leave time to do other things.

I have a huge personality. There are so many things I love to do, and each one is different in its own way. Some are physical, some are entertainment, and some are social.

Rebecca, 1993

Becca at 14 with Jake and cousins
From left: Jake, Tahli, Bria, Jayni, Zach, Aaron, Becca

Becca at 20 with Bria

Eleven

It is really true what philosophy tells us, that life must be understood backwards. But with this, one forgets the second proposition, that it must be lived forwards.
    Søren Kierkegaard, Journalen

You had found your Pegasus...

Bob and Jake and I talk about doing something special together before Jake leaves for Australia. Bob and Jake vote for a trip to Disneyland. Though that doesn't hold much appeal for me, I yield to their request. After all, nothing seems very inviting right now.

We set off at six forty-five the following morning because Jake is determined to arrive at the park before the gates open. He insists that we will stay at the park until closing time. Of course, Bob is in complete agreement. You would laugh to see how excited your twenty-year-old brother is.

I never expected that Disneyland would trigger the memories that it does, but as soon as I walk through the entrance of the park, I am flooded with images from the past. You were only four the first time Dad and I brought you here. I see your face—your mouth in a broad smile, your eyes wide as you took in all the amazing sights. You clambered on to ride after ride, ready for each new adventure. You thrilled at the colors, the sounds, the people. The memories fill me with sadness. The realization hits that this is going to be a very long and difficult day.

We walk down Main Street, past the many shops that sell Disneyland memorabilia and head for the *Indiana Jones* ride. After breezing through the short line, we tumble into the jeep that will take us on the bumpy adventure. This ride has always been one of my favorites. I do not anticipate the feelings of loss, but thoughts of your death overwhelm me.

I wonder if this is what it was like for you in the moments before the crash. When Tommie first lost control of the truck, were you tossed about the cab, jolted from one side of the seat to the other before the truck flipped over? Before that instant in which you were thrust clear of the wreckage, did the jostling and tumbling feel like this ride at Disneyland? Or was it more than this? Was it more intense, more violent, more frightening? I clench my eyes tight against the terrifying images. *Focus on the ride*, I tell myself, *not the crash, not Becca's death.* The ride comes to an end. Jake and Bob laugh as they climb out of the jeep. I am quiet, determined to hide my upset.

Thankfully, other rides in the park do not trigger me as much as *Indiana Jones*. I paste on a phony smile, determined to do everything I can to make this a pleasant day. Jake wants to go on almost every ride, even those aimed at very young children. He and Bob are ravenous for everything this day has to offer. I envy their enthusiasm.

Hours later, when they suggest another run on *Indiana Jones*, I agree, convinced that the worst is over and that I will handle the ride so much better the second time around. I am wrong. As the jeep jerks and bounces, I am bombarded with thoughts of your death and questions, so many morbid questions about what those last moments of your life were like.

* * * * *

There was very little about Disneyland that daunted you. Even at a tender age, you were quite willing to take on the rides that took you high in the air and then propelled you through treacherous curves and steep descents. Your sense of adventure was so different from my own more cautious nature. The only thing that fazed you was *Star Tours*. When you were eight, you were strenuous in your objections about the way the ride tossed you back and forth in the seat while images of outer space soared past on a movie screen. It was not that you simply disliked the ride. You were offended by it and questioned why anyone would have created such an unpleasant experience.

Jake was far more timid than you. His fear of clowns extended to a generic fear of people in costumes. That created some difficult territory for us to navigate during his first visit to the amusement park when he was two. You were set on meeting every one of the Disney characters, but your brother kept his distance. He watched your courageous approaches from afar, mesmerized by your apparent fearlessness with Snow White, Goofy, and Mickey Mouse.

Your sense of adventure was not limited to amusement parks. No, it was evident in so many aspects of your life. As a little girl, you loved to hike. You scurried over boulders with goat-like agility and easily navigated slippery rocks that provided a path across mountain streams. I was not nearly as capable as you, but you would call out words of encouragement and offer a hand to steady me as I struggled to hold my footing.

When you were in your teens, you went on a week's trip to the Sequoias with your stepsiblings and their father. You were triumphant upon your return home and announced that you had ridden horseback and mastered how to guide the horse in jumping over a log. Though I wasn't there, it is easy for me to picture you soaring through the air on the back of that horse. And in that moment, when none of the horse's hooves were touching the ground, I imagine you felt as though you were flying, airborne at last! You had found your Pegasus. What a thrill! You, my child, were always up for new adventures.

*   *   *   *   *

Work Hard, Play Hard

My family's party line is "work hard and play hard". This means that we think it is important to try very hard at school and at work. It is also very important to have fun and enjoy ourselves.

An example of this might be that I work as hard as I can in school but on the weekends it is sort of like I am a different person. I act like I really enjoy myself and have a lot of fun. Some of the things I have fun doing on the weekends are hanging out with family and friends, going to the pool and beach, and my most favorite of all, DANCING!

Dance is a combination of fun and very hard work. It is fun because I really love to move around and I also love to be graceful. It is also a great way to pass time, get energy out, and exercise. It is hard work because it is not always fun and it is so much work. I have to be focused and alert so I will be on time for the combinations.

I think it is very important to have a combination of both work and play. If I only had work that would be a very boring way to live. If I only had time where I would hang out then I probably would be sort of stupid because I would not go to school or learn. I think I have both work and play in my life.

Everyone in my family has both work and play. Even though it is very fun to hang out and play, learning and school are both very important. I guess I agree with the family line, "work hard, play hard". I am glad my family line is not just "work".

Rebecca, 1993

Twelve

We cannot conceive of what life might be like if it is not material like this life. In this life we are tied to the tangible, except our deepest experiences tend to be things that are not really physical, like love, like memory. We cannot imagine what happens after death, but the poverty of our imagination does not prove that the world is not more creative than we know.
        Rabbi David Wolpe, Making Loss Matter

I have retreated to a reality that few comprehend...

The person I used to be, the one who existed before your death, has vacated, leaving another in her stead. My physical appearance has changed. Dark circles hover below my eyes, the result of endless stretches of crying and night after night of fitful sleep. When I look in the mirror, the eyes of a stranger gaze back at me. The dull, tired stare is without life or purpose. I have to remind myself, actually say the words aloud, that the reflection is mine.

I am more fragile, vulnerable, like the delicate shell of an egg that always seems on the verge of breaking. I have so much less to say to those around me; I have retreated to a reality that

67

The heavy senseless

few comprehend. I am more forgetful, less motivated, less energetic. The heavy sense of loss does not ease. It threatens to swallow me like the whale that gulped down Jonah. The heartbreak is more constant than it was a few weeks ago. I worry that I am not dealing with your death as well as I should. Who does that, I wonder; who evaluates themselves as to whether their grieving is up to par? Still, it seems to me that I ought to be able to cope better, to function more like the person I once was, but that seems like such an impossibility. In my more rational moments, I tell myself that this is the best I can do. I am not in control of my emotions. Perhaps I am not in control of anything at all.

Next weekend is Martin Luther King's birthday; Bob is desperate to go out of town. Jake will be in Davis saying goodbye to friends. Bob reasons that this is the perfect time for us to go away. He offers up various possibilities, but I am not interested in any of them.

He tries to be patient but is frustrated by my lack of enthusiasm. He suggests Yosemite; I argue that it will be too cold there. Besides, Yosemite is a good seven hours away, and I don't want to deal with such a long time in the car. He suggests Palm Springs, but what comes to mind is boredom and a place full of old people. In an attempt to keep the peace, I offer Pismo Beach or Morro Bay, but Bob counters that we have been to those places so many times already. He proposes that we go camping. I don't want to deal with the inconvenience, the dirt, the public showers.

We agree to put the decision on hold, which means that we end up not going anywhere at all.

* * * * *

In the first weeks after your death, I felt your presence so much of the time. My life was filled with you. Do you remember the year you went off to college? We talked every day. If I wasn't home when you called, you would hang up without leaving a message on the machine. The only sign that you had called would be the blinking light on the answering machine and the steady hum of a broken connection when I went to retrieve the message. That would be my sign to call you in San Diego. Since your death, there are times when I arrive home to the blinking light on the machine but no message.

The only other person that I know of who makes a habit of calling and not leaving a message is Grandma. I have told her that every time she does this, I imagine it is you who has called. She insists that she has not done this in a very long time and promises that if she calls and I am not home, she will leave a message. I do not talk with many people about this, fretting that they will think I am crazy from grief, but the aborted messages continue. If Grandma is not making them, then who? I soothe myself with the thought that you are trying to make contact, trying to let me know that you're all right.

I am not the only one believes that you are near. Bob, Leslie, and Tahli feel your presence as well. When I do take the chance to talk about these experiences, I am easily frustrated, finding it difficult to adequately describe what is going on. These happenings do not fit into the structure of everyday perceptions. The best I can do is to approximate what it is like to feel you near.

I sense rather than feel a pressure against my chest, and that sensation takes me back to when you were an infant and I would cradle you against me. That perception of holding you brings me brief moments of peace, but those are quick to evaporate. Seconds later, your presence eludes me. I am left yearning for you again. I want the weight of you pressed to my chest. I want you to comfort me. I want us to see each other through this horrible heartbreak.

I talk out loud to you. I wander through the house and tell you what I am doing, feeling, thinking. Other times, I talk to you inside my head, without uttering a word. I am convinced that you hear me, that you know what is in my mind and heart. Still, it is not enough. I want you here like you were before you died, Rebecca.

Your death shakes my very foundation. So many things are called into question—my belief in God, life after death, how I conceive of the soul. I think back to past conversations.

"What do you think happens after we die?" you asked me.

"Something else, something more than this," I told you.

"That's what I think, too, Mom. It doesn't make sense that we just die, and there's nothing else. I believe in ghosts," you added. "I've seen them."

"You have?" I said.

"Yeah. The house around the corner is haunted, but the ghosts there don't do anything bad. Sometimes I even think there are ghosts here in our house. Do you believe in God? I do. I'm not sure what God is exactly, but I know there is one."

We went on to talk about souls and the purpose of life, spending hours trying to untangle the mysteries of the universe. You yearned for answers, and I tried to encourage you in your search. How ironic that now I am the one who is searching.

I have started back in therapy, choosing to again work with Maggie since she helped us through the divorce and some of your adolescent struggles. I reason that by working with her, I won't have to recreate our entire family story. I try to convince myself that talking with her is a productive and a healthy response to your death, but in the end it does little to comfort me. After half a dozen sessions, I pull out of therapy, having concluded that I can get as much help from talking with close friends. The truth is that no one can make this pain stop; no one fully understands what it is like to lose you.

Picture a woman who is far along in her pregnancy, her womb round and ripe with life, her face glowing with the anticipation of this new child she is bringing into the world. Now, hollow out her belly and in its stead put emptiness, darkness. That is me. That is my world. How can anything lessen this horrific pain?

It is a little over a month since your death. Bob and I are the only ones at home. My sleep has been fitful, but tonight I fall asleep without struggle. Somewhere around two in the morning, I awaken to the sound of footsteps creaking against the board at the top of the stairs. When you were a teenager, this was the same noise that told me you were trying to slip in unnoticed long after curfew. I do not worry about an intruder being in the house. Instead, I listen to the sound and think about you. When the noise disappears, I drift back to sleep, having found some solace in your footsteps.

It is not until Bob and I are eating breakfast that I remember the night's sounds. I ask him whether he has heard them. He tells me that he has.

"I didn't want to wake you," he says. "I thought you were asleep. The footsteps are nothing to worry about."

"I know," I respond. "They are Becca's."

"Yes," he agrees.

The following night, Bob is up late. When he does fall asleep, he snores, making it impossible for me to get any rest. By one-thirty, I retreat to the living room couch where I burrow under blankets. Footsteps and the creaking of the floorboard float down to me. Is Bob awake, perhaps going to the bathroom or heading down to cajole me back to bed? The noise stops, and then I feel you up against me. I turn on my side and hold you close, taking comfort from your presence. Much later, I fall asleep, but the next morning when I awaken, you are gone.

Over breakfast, I ask Bob if he was up during the night, but he tells me no, that once he fell asleep he stayed asleep. Three loud thuds from up above interrupt our conversation.

"Probably the oranges falling off the tree," I say to him, considering the large tree that hangs out over the family room from the neighbor's yard.

Bob shakes his head. "The oranges aren't ripe enough yet." He looks out the window to the backyard. "There isn't any wind, nothing to cause the oranges to drop."

I offer to go upstairs to make sure that there isn't someone on the roof trying to get into the house.

"There's no one up there," he insists. "Leave it alone. If anyone was there, we would see their shadow out in the yard." He shrugs. "Maybe it's Becca."

When I talk with Aunt Leslie about the noises in the house, she tells me that she does not believe that you were ready to die, not ready to let go any more than I was. "Becca wants to be here with you," she says.

Her words make sense. Both you and I expected years and years that we would spend together. I treasure the memories and the visits from the other side, Rebecca, but they are not enough to sustain me. They do not make up for the fact that you have died. They are not substitutes for having you here in the flesh, here in this world with me where you belong.

*   *   *   *   *

The Colors of Me

I can be the radiant yellow sunshine
On a hot August day
Glowing, energetic,
Bright, and full of life,
Bursting with laughter
As I joke with friends

Yet sometimes I am
Mellow, pensive
Hesitant to show emotion,
Hiding, like the periwinkle streaks,
In the sky at dusk

I am a contrast of feeling and color,
But if you could take
A ray of the sun
And a piece of the sky
There I would be
           Rebecca, January 30, 1997

Thirteen

Every blade of grass has its angel that bends over it and whispers,
"Grow, grow."
        Talmud, Midrash Rabba, Bereshit 10:6

The words leave me wishing that in those last moments before your
death, your angels had been able to sweep you up and keep you safe...

Two others died in the crash; that's what I keep thinking. I
want to know about these young men. Who were they when
they were alive? I need physical descriptions, information
about their interests, their passions. Were they close to you or
only casual acquaintances? I don't know if it is possible to get
any answers.

It is disconcerting to think that you spent your last hours
with these two and that I never even met them. Would
knowing who Mike and Tim were in the world help me make
sense out of all this chaos? Probably not. Still, I want the
information. I want faces to link to the names. I grab on to bits
of information that circle in from friends and acquaintances.

Of course you know that Mike and Tim were first
cousins. From what I hear, they grew up in a tight-knit

extended family not unlike ours. Tim's parents are ranchers. I picture Tim in worn Levi's, envision him as tall and slender and brown from the sun. Mike was an athlete. Many say that he was quite accomplished in baseball. I picture him as broad and stocky, his face square. I imagine his complexion lighter than Tim's. Did I see photos in the obituary section of the newspaper? I'm not sure. And then there is the other image that I have to shove away—Tim and Mike lying in caskets, and you in yours.

I consider contacting their parents, imagine sitting down over tea with the surviving mothers. I play out the conversation we would have. Would sharing our pain bring comfort? When I tell mutual acquaintances of my idea to get in touch with these women, they discourage me. They point out that Tim and Mike's mothers are in their own world of pain and do not want to meet me. As time goes on, it becomes clear that legal concerns may be a factor in these women not wanting to talk with me. The truck that Tommie was driving that night belonged to one of the other boys' fathers. Perhaps these families' attorneys have instructed them to keep their distance. My curiosity does not easily recede. Weeks later, I wonder what these grieving mothers look like, where they live. If they are coping, are they surviving better than I am? Can I learn from them and find some relief from my agony?

More information comes in. Tim's parents live out past the Temple on Foothill—a short distance from the crash site. I file that away in my brain, another brief note about the surviving families. I track down the address as well as that for Mike's parents. And then, when I am by myself, I set out.

The day is sunny with only a few clouds in the sky. It is early afternoon, so there isn't much traffic, which means that in less than ten minutes I am turning on to Mike's street. It is an upper-middle-class neighborhood, much like ours. Well-maintained houses stand on both sides of the quiet tree-lined street. There is no one in sight. Though it is a weekday, I wonder if Mike's mother is at home and if so, what she is doing. Is she thinking about her son? Is she wandering around the house trying to find something to occupy her? Is she sitting in his room, sifting through his belongings? Does she search for hidden treasures, reminders of her son? I scan the addresses and finally locate the correct one. I do not stop, do not go up to the house. I drive back and forth a couple of times and slow to a crawl to catch a glimpse of what? The color of their home, the plants that decorate the yard, the type of cars they own, anything that might offer a clue as to who these people are.

Once I have had my fill, I leave the neighborhood and drive less than a mile past the Temple up Foothill. As I head east on the two-lane stretch, housing tracts give way to sloping hills to the north and small ranches and citrus groves to the south. Driving this road used to provide me with an escape from the congestion of town. Now, it is a brutal reminder of your death.

The bumper sticker on the car in front of me captures my attention. It reads: *Never drive faster than your angels can fly.* The words leave me wishing that in those last moments before your death, your angels had been able to sweep you up and keep you safe. Why didn't they caution you to be more careful? *Never drive faster than your angels can fly.* Would you have listened, recognized the danger? Would you have believed that Tommie's truck was a deathtrap?

As I approach Tim's parents' house, I slow and search for something that will tell me more about this family. There is nothing. Only a quiet secluded place outside the city limits, the kind of place I always thought would be wonderful to live. I turn the car around and cruise by one more time. How sad it must be for these people to live out on this stretch, to know that this is the same path their son took the night he died. At least in my world, I can avoid this place.

I head home without answers. All I have learned is that these families live in rather ordinary places, much like me.

Their lives have most likely been filled with the usual passions and struggles, at least until Thanksgiving morning when the three of you died.

* * * * *

When I grow up I want to be a doctor. The reason why I want to be a doctor is I want to help people and I think it would be neat to see how people's bodies work and what kinds of sicknesses there are and how to cure them. I would also like to be a dancer part of the time because I really like to dance on stage. I also really like to sing a lot too. I took a lot of dance classes and I've been in a lot of plays and shows. I would also like to be a mother and have three kids—two girls and one boy. I really wish I could be a famous dancer. I also really wish I could marry a man that was a dentist.

Rebecca, November 5, 1991

Fourteen

Say not in grief "she is no more" but in thankfulness that she was.
  Jewish Proverb

I curl my fingers a bit, as though I am holding your hand in mine...

Determined to hold on to the memories, I handle them with care. I imagine them as a precious liquid that I cup in the palm of my hand, one that might disappear with a single misstep or stumble. I am still able to hear your voice. I remember the peal of laughter that could fill the house or the way your words would rise in anger and frustration as you struggled to get me to see your side of an argument. With the passing of time, I worry that bits and pieces of you will fade away. Will there come a day when I will no longer be able to remember? Will the subtle nuances fall away? I shiver at the thought.

Pictures and videotapes that chronicle your childhood are packed away in the family room cupboards. Your poems, essays, and artwork are tucked in a large cardboard box that sits under my desk upstairs. Your diary is secreted away in the depths of your closet along with other treasures. What I do not have, what I so desperately need, is a recording of your voice. My memory is the only place where I can find that precious cadence. And that feels too tenuous, too unreliable. I see my mind like a well-worn piece of fabric that is thread bare and frayed around the edges. How can it possibly support these essential memories?

In my quest for reassurance, I phone Rabbi Lisa and set up an appointment to meet with her. I confess my fear and tell her about the sense of urgency to preserve everything about you. She does little to console me. Instead, she tells me that I will indeed forget some things. I want to rage at her. I want her to reassure me that everything will be all right. I need her to promise that I'll be able to hold on to my memories, that I will remember everything about you, always.

Rabbi Lisa's calm, even-keeled voice reels me in. "You'll remember what you need to," she says. "But there will be some things about Rebecca that you'll forget. As time goes by, you are going to let go of some of the memories."

No! I need to remember everything! I tell myself that she doesn't know what she's talking about, that she can't possibly understand the depth of my grief. But that is a lie. Having lost both her parents when she was a young woman, she understands grief all too well. Her words come from her heart, from a place of compassion and experience.

I consider the next half of my life and the oppressive span of time that lies ahead without you here. So many moments will be different because of your death, Rebecca. Jake will graduate from college and become a rabbi, but you will not be there to share in the joy. He will get married, have children. But you won't be a part of those celebrations. You won't get to hold your niece or nephew or entertain them with stories about the escapades of the Singer cousins. You won't have the opportunity to tell them about what it was like for you and Jake growing up together.

I will be there, though. I promise that I will tell the next generation about their aunt who died way before her time. I will tell them every story I can remember. I will give them as much of you as I possibly can. It won't be enough, though. I know that. But at least it is something. When I recount the stories to my grandchildren, I will mourn for you all over again. And I will be so sad that these children will not get to experience you firsthand. You would have made a terrific aunt, Becca. You would have been the one the children turned to for excitement, for laughter, for heart-to-heart talks that they could not have with anybody else. It's not fair, you know. None of this is.

*   *   *   *   *

"When I'm grown and have children of my own, things are going to be my way," you announced. "You're going to have to follow my lead as to how I want to raise my children, Mom."

I waited for you to expound on how I had been overly strict and too protective of you and your brother when you were growing up. I was sure that you would tell me you were going to give your children more freedom, be less cautious and neurotic than I've been.

So I was surprised when you said, "There are going to be more rules when I'm a parent. My children aren't going to get away with things the way I have. They're going to know what's expected of them. If they do something wrong, there will be consequences. I'm not going to give them second chances when it comes to important stuff. I'm smarter than you were about some things.

"You were such a good kid, Mom, so you didn't expect me to experiment with things," you went on. "My kids aren't going to get away with any of that. But I'm not going to make them afraid of life, either. I want them to experience the world, to know that they can handle problems."

"Sounds like a decent plan," I agreed. "I'm sure you'll make a wonderful mother."

"Do you think you'll be able to accept the way I want things done?" you asked.

"Sure," I said, anticipating that you would mellow by the time I became a grandmother.

"Good," you said, "I thought you'd have a hard time with me being in charge and making the rules."

"Maybe I'll surprise you."

You laughed and shrugged your shoulders. "Maybe."

*   *   *   *   *

You seem even more present than you have in recent weeks. Bob and I hear your footsteps around the house, typically when we are upstairs watching television or lying in bed waiting for sleep. I have been seeing peripheral flashes of light and movement. Bob and Aunt Leslie have had similar experiences. Late at night, I feel you pressed against my chest, cuddling in against me. I am comforted to have you here with me. I try to be content with your presence.

I go for an early morning walk. The air is cold and heavy with moisture, the sunlight bright and startling. I whisper a prayer of thanks for these blessings and am overcome with the profound sense that you are here with me. You are so close, so real. I curl my fingers a bit, as though I am holding your hand in mine. Your presence evokes tears and smiles. I think about your sense of humor, your quick temper, and your endless stream of chatter.

Once home, I head upstairs. I stare at the pictures on your bedroom walls and think about how much care you took in designing this space. You deliberated about the color for the walls, finally settling on blue. But then the decision became what shade of blue—light or dark, with or without a hint of green or purple. You asked for my help in figuring out the placement of furniture and pictures, experimenting with one setup and then the next, then returning to the initial one again. I love how this room reflects you, Bec. You decided on a lovely shade of pale aqua for the walls. There is a photo of a lone figure walking with umbrella in hand down a sepia-colored bridge. It speaks to you being an independent thinker, someone who wanted to be her own person. In another picture, a golden wave creates a hollow tunnel of light as the ocean water hovers for a moment before its inevitable tumble toward shore. This reminds me about your love of the ocean and your questions about the universe and creation.

Your bookshelf is filled with photographs. Two of the pictures capture you and me at your graduation. I drink in our happy smiles. I hope you understood how very proud I was of you. In the other photo, I am planting a kiss on your beaming face. We are frozen in time, mother and daughter on graduation day. My gaze wanders to a picture of you with your stepmother and stepsister, and another of you with friends. I run my finger across a photo of you and your cousins settled on the family room couch. You orchestrated that shot during a recent Hanukah celebration, directing your cousins where to sit. As my finger slides across your image, I imagine that I am touching the soft mocha-colored skin of your face. I tell you how dear you are to me. You are my girl, you know. That never changes.

I open your closet and press my nose against your clothing. I breathe in your scent—perfume, soap, musty incense. Your lingering smell is one of life's blessings. A friend tells me that when her husband died, she packed away a couple of his socks in a plastic bag just to preserve his smell. Linda sometimes opens that bag in order to remember Craig's fragrance.

Perhaps I should do the same, try to lock away your essence and save it for as long as possible. Will your scent be one of the things that I forget? I don't think so. A mother cannot possibly forget the smell of her child. That is embedded in the deepest recesses of my mind.

That first year we had together, I inhaled your perfume every chance I had. I nuzzled my nose against the soft curve of your neck, pressed my face against your belly, snuggled up close to you and drank in the aroma of your freshly shampooed hair.

You were always so sensitive to smells. By the time you were two years old, you often insisted on climbing up on a kitchen chair to explore the spice jars that were far out of your reach. I would take one down and then another and another and then unscrew the lids so that you could get a whiff of the aromatic herbs and spices. You identified them all, astounding me with your accuracy every time we played the game.

Your heightened sense of smell endured over the years, making you a discerning judge of almost anything that had an odor. You rarely kept your opinions to yourself. Whoever was within earshot knew whether or not a smell met with your approval. I could be cooking dinner downstairs while you were otherwise occupied in a far off corner of the house. You would call to me and either applaud the aroma or dismiss it with disdain. Flowers, perfumes, even the lingering hint of someone having been in the bathroom, were all fair game. How I would love now to catch a glimpse of you turning up your nose at some offending odor or see the trace of a smile sweeping across your face as you breathed in a pleasing scent.

I remain in your room for well over an hour and watch the changing play of light as the sun dips beneath the horizon. The vivid colors of late afternoon fall away to deepening shadows, eventually leaving me in total darkness. I remain on your bed, propped up against your pillows. I pull my knees in close to my chest and circle my arms around them. The air grows chilly. I wrap myself in your tiger-striped fleece blanket and find some solace in the dark cave of your room.

Bob will not be home for another hour. I have plenty of

time to immerse myself in memories and solitude. Tonight, I let the memories take me where they will, rolling me back and forth across the years. The memories propel me forward into the present and then sweep me back to the past. Back and forth, back and forth like ocean waves. Their rise and fall takes me on a tender journey through time and helps me to survive the sorrow.

*   *   *   *   *

Of My Sorrow

Sorrow sweeps over me
bathes me in its wind-washed essence
its ebb and flow constantly changes
and I wonder if it, too, is governed
by the movement of heavenly bodies

My sorrow is a part of me
as familiar as the rising of the sun
and the night's heavy darkness
it is steady, stubborn
unyielding

I live in its presence
in its shadow.
Reanne, December 14, 2004

*   *   *   *   *

If I had another week of vacation, I would spend more time with my family. This is because I feel like I didn't really see them much because I was dancing, and hanging out with my friends, and doing homework, and a few other things. My family is really important to me and I want to spend more time with them but lately I haven't had any extra time. Homework has been taking me a very long time every day. With that and dancing I don't really have time for a life or my family. I want more time with my family because it is important to be with your family so that you can have a good relationship as you get older. A way this could change would be not to have as much homework, especially on the weekends. I am frustrated because there is nothing I can do about this. I can't change how much homework I get. Even during vacation I had homework. That was even more frustrating.

Rebecca, January 3, 1995

Reanne with Becky at the beach

Becca at 20 with Reanne

Fifteen

May God bless you and keep you;
May God's face to shine upon you and be gracious to you;
May God lift up His countenance upon you and give you peace.
  Numbers 6:24-26

Time moves in a slow, torturous progression...

Life means change. I know that, and yet, I fight against those changes, much preferring the comfort that comes with predictability. But life is not like that. It unfolds with a will all its own.

When I was growing up in Los Angeles, there was an amusement park on the Santa Monica Pier. The park was surrounded on three sides by the Pacific Ocean, with a Ferris wheel that soared up into the sky. In truth, the amusement park was very small, but I didn't think of it that way. I found it impressive with its grand assortment of rides and booths.

The *House of Mirrors* was one of my favorite stops. I remember being about eight years old and entering the maze through a narrow doorway that took me into an eerie, dimly lit land of make-believe. Threading my way through a series of snaking corridors, I walked through room after room that seemed off kilter. One space produced the illusion of being far too large and expansive, while another was cramped and terribly tiny. In retrospect, I am sure the intent was to mimic what Alice had experienced in Wonderland. Other rooms were lined with warped mirrors that altered my appearance. In one room, I seemed to become elongated and thin. In another, I was short and squat. None of this frightened me. I had been through the *House of Mirrors* many times and knew what to expect. Besides, I understood these changes were only temporary distortions. The exit would take me back out into the sunlight and the waiting arms of my parents. Had I thought that the transformations were permanent, I would have been terrified.

Now, I find myself in the midst of a very different reality, one in which I have no control. Life has swallowed me whole, cornered me in a treacherous *House of Mirrors* from which there is no escape. I am along for the ride, trying my best to hold on to who I am. Your death has been the ultimate challenge and has forced me into changes that I never would have chosen.

The next transition is upon us—Jake's departure for Australia. He is scheduled to leave this evening. I brace for the changes his leaving will surely bring. My selfish inclination is to keep Jake here with me, but I have to balance that against the knowledge that this year abroad will be amazing for him. What an opportunity! I am not about to deny him this adventure. It will be difficult to have him so far away, but we will somehow survive the separation.

Time moves in a slow, torturous progression as I await the inevitable goodbyes. Tears hover below the surface. I push them down, once again wanting to protect Jake from my emotions. If I cry, that will only make his departure more difficult. Besides, if I give in to the sadness, there will be no end to it. I am sure of that.

Wanting to capture as much time as I can with your

brother, I have taken the day off work. I shadow him as he goes about his preparations and then busy myself around the house so as not to be too intrusive. When I walk past Jake's room, he is packing the last odds and ends for the trip. I light on the edge of his bed as he shoves one more shirt and a final pair of pants into the already over-stuffed suitcase. The two of us make small talk that seems more important, more crucial than it would be in any other circumstance. We try to cram in as many words as possible before Jake leaves.

Evening approaches, and we are subdued. Bob's arrival home signals that even more time has slipped away. Dinner is all that remains before your father comes to drive Jake to the airport. I wander from room to room in search of some distraction from my sadness and anxiety. I ask your brother if there is anything else he needs. Has he remembered to pack his passport, his traveler's checks? Bob questions whether Jake has enough cash. Ignoring your brother's protests, he presses money into your brother's hand.

As we sit down to an early dinner, my throat constricts. There is no point in trying to eat. Jake and Bob have a light, hurried meal. There are hugs and repeated proclamations about how much we will all miss each other. I tell Jake that I love him, that I am proud of him. There is an urgency to everything we say. I remind him to call us as soon as he lands in Australia. I caution him to stay safe, to avoid any unnecessary risks. He makes a solemn promise. How am I going to bear having him so far away?

Then your father is at the front door. Bob and Jake hoist heavy suitcases and walk to the car with me trailing behind. Bob hugs your brother, which makes me all the more emotional. I dig a nail into the palm of my hand to calm myself. Your father and I remain quiet and exchange looks that acknowledge the pain we are both feeling. Bob lets go of Jake; it is my turn to say goodbye. It is in that moment of Bob releasing your brother that I realize this is the last time that I will be able to hold Jake close for an entire year. I wrap my arms around him and inhale the scent of his aftershave. Jake trembles against me. We are both in tears.

"I love you," I tell him.

"I love you, too," he says.

Terrified at the thought of sending him off halfway around the world, I ask God to protect him. Does God understand that I cannot survive losing two children? Jake and I loosen our hold. He disappears inside your father's car.

Bob and I are frozen, arm in arm, as we watch the car move down the street. I blow a kiss after your brother and bury my face into Bob's shoulder. Harsh, gut-wrenching spasms overtake me as the car disappears around the corner. I want to run after them. I want to tell your brother not to go, to stay here with me.

"He'll be just fine," Bob assures me.

From your lips to God's ears, I want to say, but the sobs have rendered me mute.

Life has taken me down a very unexpected path. I am alone with one child dead and the other traveling to the far side of the globe. Today, it is easy to feel sorry for myself, to be consumed by sadness. I hate this *House of Mirrors* in which I find myself.

Bob and I retreat into the empty house and begin the year-long wait for your brother's safe return.

*   *   *   *   *

You

You are the one remaining
the vessel for my hopes and dreams
your face, your smile
now speak for both of you

You are the one who holds my future
my legacy
I look to you for grandchildren
for a way to preserve my name
my memories, my stories

You are the one remaining
you are my light
my heart…
you

         Reanne, December 9, 2004

*   *   *   *   *

    The ocean is nice and when I see it makes me feel great. If we didn't have the ocean there wouldn't be any whales or dolphins or other creatures under the water. It would be neat to see under water. I've seen pictures on TV or in a movie but I think it would be really neat to go scuba diving and see what's really down there for myself. I really love the animals and the ocean under there.

    Rebecca, September 13, 1991

Sixteen

The one who does not search will not find. The one who does not search will lose anew, for he will have lost not only the person but the complex of meaning and the richness of memory that the person leaves behind.

  Rabbi David Wolpe, Making Loss Matter

I struggle to unravel all that went on in the months before your death...

Two months after your death, I call the Highway Patrol for an update on your case. No charges have been filed nor has the report been sent to the District Attorney's office. It is in the hands of a sergeant and is being proofed. When I ask about the toxicology report on Tommie, I'm told that the information cannot be released yet. I am left frustrated and impatient.

So many unanswered questions about the crash. I assume that Tommie had too much to drink that night, but did you as well? Was your judgment impaired? You knew better than to get in a car with someone who had been drinking; we'd certainly talked about that. And you knew better than to ride in a car without a seat belt. When you were small, you would insist that we belt in your doll and your pretend friend. *Dididee* and *Justidee*—do you remember them?

I talk with one of my colleagues about your death. Cindy tells me that her children are about your age and frequent some of the same places where you and your friends used to go. Her eyes are moist as she discloses that one of her children's friends was at the bar that night.

"He talked with some of the people who were there with Rebecca," she says. "He told some of the guys they weren't in any shape to drive and offered that they could sleep at his place since he only lives a few blocks from the bar."

I draw in a breath and wait to see what else she knows.

"They told him they were fine and then drove off in the truck. My daughter's friend says he wishes he had done something more to intervene. I'm so sorry. It could have been any of our kids that night. God, it could have been any of us."

There are those words again, reassuring me, comforting me.

"We've all done stupid things," Cindy continues, wiping her eyes. "We were lucky enough to survive. Becky wasn't. It's so sad that she didn't have the time and the opportunity to grow up. She would have, you know; she would have made better decisions." She forces a thin smile before hugging me. "I'm sure of that. Becky would have been fine. She was just going through a phase; so many kids do."

I want to believe her. God how I want that.

"We tell our kids not to drive drunk. We caution them about the dangers, but how often do we think to tell them not to ride with someone who's been drinking? We figure they know that." She sighs. "The kids think they're invincible. They think they have it all figured out. It's too easy for them to get into danger and then..." She gestures in a wide circle with her arm as if searching for what more to say. "I'm so sorry it ended this way. You were a good mother. This was just a terrible accident."

*   *   *   *   *

Like most young adults, you lived a life that was quite separate from that of your parents. There were people you knew, places you went, of which I had no knowledge. I knew only as much as you were willing to share with me. The rest was speculation. Now I need to understand it all. I struggle to unravel all that went on in the months before your death.

Your twenty-second year was full of questions. You were trying to figure out who you were in the world. Your long-term relationship with David was less than stable. You took it hard when the relationship came to an end a few months before your death. You were working full time and planning to go back to school, entertaining the idea of becoming a nurse. Despite the confidence you tried so hard to project, you were young and unsure of yourself.

It is late Sunday afternoon when your high school friend, Daena, stops by the house to offer her condolences. This is the first time since the funeral that I have seen her. Perhaps this is an opportunity to have some of my questions answered.

Daena has never been very comfortable with Bob or me. Today, she seems even more ill-at-ease than usual. She follows Bob to the kitchen where she stumbles through stilted greetings. He motions her to a nearby chair at the dining room table.

"I'm sorry," she says, beginning to cry. "I can't do this. I haven't been in the house since…" Her voice fades.

"It's all right," I say, surprised that I am consoling her.

Daena shakes her head. "I need to leave." She reaches into her purse and retrieves an envelope which she thrusts into my hand. "I'm really sorry." She pulls herself to her feet.

"Why don't you sit down for a few minutes?" Bob suggests. "Don't leave like this."

She reluctantly eases back down.

"I'll heat some water for tea," he offers.

Daena nods and nervously pulls at a cuticle. Struggling to contain the tears, she looks over at me. "I don't know what to say to you. This is so difficult."

"It's okay to cry," I tell her.

"I don't do that very much." She shakes her head. "I keep my feelings at a distance. But being here in this house brings it all up." She sniffles and dabs at her eyes. "I wrote you a card." She points to the envelope that's now sitting between us on the table. "But don't open it. Do that later, after I leave." She draws in an unsteady breath. "It doesn't seem real, you know. I was here the week before she died. Do you remember? I spent the night, and Becky and I stayed awake late, giggling and talking. The next morning, we all had breakfast together. Bec and I made crepes for you and Bob."

"I remember," I say, thinking back to how unusually comfortable Daena had seemed that day.

Bob brings three mugs of tea to the table. I gratefully wrap my hands around the warm cup. Daena stirs honey into hers. I wait to see if there's something more she wants to say. We exchange memories of you and tell each other about our sadness and grief. I don't cry. I don't want to scare Daena off by becoming too emotional. I ask her what she knew about your relationship with David and why the two of you broke up, but she doesn't seem to have any answers. I ask how much time you were spending with Tommie, but she doesn't know that either.

As I watch her leave, I am struck by how young she is, twenty-two. Her life continues on while yours has been cut short. What are those pangs I'm feeling—confusion, bitterness at the unfairness of all this? Maybe I'm a bit envious as well. At some point, Daena's grief will ease, but mine never will. Your death is part of me. Embedded in everything that defines me, it weaves through my soul, creating an unrelenting tapestry of sorrow. I need to learn to live with that. I need to learn how to exist alongside the heartbreak.

*   *   *   *   *

Still unsettled, I want to know more about what was going on in your life right before your death. Everything about you, every detail of your life is now something precious that I must hold on to. But is this searching, this questioning, a way to convince myself that I have some control? I delude myself into believing that if I can make sense out of your life and death, if I can understand enough, then perhaps I can undo what has happened and bring you back to life. I know, magical thinking. But it is where I am right now.

Determined to reclaim the parts of you that you kept private, I call one of your friends who is away at school in Berkeley. We talk about your breakup with David. Kori believes that when David was in the Navy and stationed overseas, it was convenient for him to have you as a girlfriend. Once he came home and was faced with making an adult commitment, the relationship served less of a purpose. I am struck by her insight. I ask her about your relationship with Tommie. She indicates that she isn't even sure if the two of you were dating.

"Tommie wasn't settled," she observes. "He wasn't in a good place in his life. He didn't have a direction. Tending bar isn't a great job. I told Becky to wait, told her that if the two of them were meant to be together, the relationship would be there later on."

I ask Kori about the weekend when you and Tommie went up to visit her.

"We had a good time," she explains. "It was clear that Tommie and Becky really cared for one another, but I don't think they were together back then, not as boyfriend and girlfriend. I adored Becky. She was the best friend anyone could ever hope for. She would do anything to help me, but..." She hesitates. "There were times when I knew she wasn't being completely truthful with me, and I don't understand why. It's

97

sad that she felt like she had to hide things from the people who cared about her."

Her observation hits me hard because it is something that I have experienced with you as well. Feeling compelled to help her understand, I wonder about my need to defend you and excuse your behaviour. I tell Kori of your concerns about what people thought of you. We talk about the difficulty you had with school and the insecurities you experienced around the issue of being adopted. From my perspective, you never wholly believed you fit in. Like Daena, Kori has less information about your struggles and choices than I do.

When I tell my sisters about my conversations with your friends, they remind me that you were only twenty-two when you died, still a kid in so many ways. You were in the process of forming your identity and deciding on a direction for your life. The breakup with David created even more questions as to where and how you fit into the world. When Tommie appeared on the scene and expressed an interest in you, it must have been an enticing invitation. Would the outcome have been different if you had been more self-assured, more at ease with yourself? Would you still be alive if you had been more sure of who you were in the world? I am left to wonder.

*   *   *   *   *

If the Yearbook Was Real

What is the yearbook?
Is it all good or all bad?
Or a war between both?
What would we see if our masks were all gone?
What would we fear if we were revealed?

The yearbook now.
Fly through the pages.
People laughing, happy,
Everything grand.
Good grades,
People achieving,
Senior best,
Popular,
Beautiful,
Intelligent,
All around great.
Perfect couples,
Mighty football players,
Flawless cheerleaders.

Snap!
Back to reality.
Intolerance,
Kids being judged,
Peer pressure,
Turning to drugs,
Grades going down,
Gangs,
Competition,
Fighting in the halls.

If the yearbook was real,
What would we see when the masks were all gone?
      Rebecca, February 10, 1996

Seventeen

"Last forever!" Who hasn't prayed that prayer? ...The present is a freely given canvas. That it is constantly being ripped apart and washed downstream goes without saying.
    Annie Dillard, Pilgrim at Tinker Creek

I pray that the end came fast...

With your brother in Australia, I am now faced with even more time alone. The multiple phone calls to Jake each week are only a temporary salve for my loneliness. I love hearing about his life in Melbourne, but that doesn't ease the pain of having him so far away. I am reminded once again that I am a mother without her children.

Bob limits his clients to daytime hours; but even with this, there are long, difficult hours when I am on my own. I trail from room to room and listen to the sounds that used to fill this house. I hear you calling to me, trying to get my attention in order to tell me something you have just remembered. The ring of your laughter mixes with that of your brother's, sounds from the past that follow me through this space that has now become empty and hollowed out. Jake is on the other side of the world and you, Rebecca, are even further away, somewhere I can only try to imagine. The peals of laughter are simply memories. This place that used to be filled with your voice, with Jake's, has been rendered silent. *This is what death is*, I think to myself—*unwanted silence, cold and impenetrable silence.*

Your death makes no sense. I try to soothe myself by pretending that you have not died. I delude myself into believing that you will be home soon. I only have to be patient. But you don't come, and I am left to roam the silent rooms. I try to convince myself that understanding what took place the night your life ended will bring me some peace. But will it? Can it move me any closer to accepting this horror?

Was your death the price you paid for going along with your friends? You so wanted to fit in. You worried whether your friends thought you were smart enough, funny enough, interesting enough. I suppose that those are questions most of us ask during adolescence and early adulthood. As your mother, I wished you could see yourself with more compassion and realism. I wanted you to believe in the vivacious, charming girl with the big heart and quick wit. I wanted you to have at least a taste of the way so many others experienced you. You were able to rattle off your positive traits, but never fully embraced them, concluding that you were fooling those who saw the best in you.

The night of the crash, you were out with Tommie. The high school romance that had fizzled more than once had more recently started up again. Your relationship seemed to leave you perplexed, questioning what it was you wanted in life and whether Tommie would be able to help you get there.

Four other friends of Tommie's joined you that evening. I don't imagine that it would have been easy for you to go against such a crowd. Your insecurities made you all the more susceptible to peer pressure. Late that night, when the group decided to go to a bar, you probably felt compelled to go as well. And when they left the bar to return to the ranch where Tommie and Tim both lived, it would have been difficult for you to refuse to get in the truck with them. I can picture the crew piling into the pickup without a care and directing you to sit on the front console between Tommie and Mike.

"It's a short ride to the ranch," they would have told you. "It's late. There's no one on the road at this hour."

Nestling in between the two men, you must have deluded yourself with a false sense of safety. If you had any doubts about what you were doing, those would have been silenced by your concern as to how it would look to remain behind and call your parents for a ride home. Not only would you get an earful from your friends, you would also be worried about the lecture you figured would follow from Bob and me. So you climbed into the truck, ready for the next adventure of the evening, fully expecting there to be more conversation and laughter before everyone headed home.

Besides, you often saw yourself as indestructible. That, coupled with your stubborn assertiveness, put you in even more danger. Remember the arguments we used to have about what you were doing, where you were going and with whom? I still think about an evening last year when you took off on foot to meet some friends a few blocks away at a café near the college. You refused a ride from Bob or me, preferring instead to enjoy the night air and a solitary walk. I told you that you were taking unnecessary risks, putting yourself in harm's way. You saw me as neurotic and overprotective and insisted you would be fine on your own.

Yes, I know, I was overprotective. I admit that. And growing up, I took far fewer chances than you did. My innocence coupled with your rebellious nature were one hell of a combination.

When you were younger, I used to caution you to be careful. Years later, the family would tease me about telling you and your brother and cousins: *don't do that, you could fall and hit your head, you might have to go to the hospital, you could die*—one of those things that parents say and then wish that they could take back. But back then I meant those words. I was so afraid that something awful would happen to you. Now it has.

The night before Thanksgiving, Tommie navigated the well-lit roads that lead toward the foothills. He steered the truck onto the two-lane ribbon that winds along the base of the hills between Ventura and Santa Paula. With no street lights to illuminate the way, it must have been incredibly dark out there. The only thing surrounding you would have been blackness and wide expanses of shadowy orchards and ranch land.

Tommie was right; there were very few cars on the road. He pressed down on the gas, accelerating beyond the speed limit. People go fast on that road, so why not him as well? Things probably went fine until he came out of a turn and caught the dirt shoulder off to the right with the tires. He would have attempted to correct the mistake, but then pulled the wheel too hard, too fast. The truck veered across the middle of the road. Tommie fought to control the sudden turn of the truck. There are skid marks out there that attest to that. Until that point, I imagine you were laughing and talking with your friends. I can picture the way you might have jerked your head up to find the truck on the wrong side of the road. Perhaps you glanced over at Tommie and caught the sudden change of expression, the look of shock and concern that clouded his face.

And then the truck flipped over—once, twice, maybe even three times, tossing you around the cab like a rag doll. You must have screamed, your voice swallowed up in the panicked shouts of your friends. You and Tim were thrown from the truck. It is too disturbing to imagine the mechanics of you being propelled out of the cab. Sadness and panic threaten to swallow me as I think of you ending up a number of feet below the road on a rocky embankment. Try as I might, I cannot escape the violence of the crash, the sudden loss of control, the shattering glass as the truck collided with the pavement.

My breathing is labored. I can't get enough air into my lungs. And I'm shaking, shivering with cold. Over and over again, I see you sailing out of the truck, flying through the dark night. How I wish I could have been there to catch you, Rebecca. How I wish I could have kept you safe.

So many unanswered questions, all the what-ifs. If only you had made a different decision. What if Tommie hadn't been drinking that night? What if you hadn't gotten in the truck with him? What if a doctor had been on the scene and had been able to provide you with immediate medical attention? Would you be alive now? Yes, I know, I'm perfectly capable of driving myself crazy with all the unknowns.

Keep telling yourself it lasted for only a few seconds, I whisper, as though this is my own private prayer. Reassure yourself that Becky went sailing out of the cab of the truck like one of her cherished fairies. I try to console myself with the belief that you went quickly. I need to believe that you hardly had time to know what was happening. You couldn't have had more than a brief moment in which you realized that you were in danger. Then it was over. There was silence and your soul moving upward, into the light, into the night and whatever lies beyond.

I pray that the end came fast, my love. I pray that you didn't know what was happening, that you weren't aware of the cold, dark night that surrounded you. I pray that you didn't hear the wind howling through the ravine like the lonesome cry of a coyote. Holding fast to the hope that you had a swift, easy death keeps me sane. It is too painful, too frightening to imagine it any other way.

*   *   *   *   *

Who Is Rebecca?

After talking to my friends, family members, teachers and classmates I have come to the conclusion that many people perceive me in the same way that I perceive myself. Many people see me as a person with very high morals. This includes being very involved with family, being non-materialistic, and responsible. People who are close to me know that I have very strong ideas and am very opinionated. However, I do not consistently express my ideas unless asked. People around me understand that I am my own person and know that I am not easily influenced by other people. These same people might say that I would never do something just because others are or because I was told to. Also, I am not afraid to take a chance and be creative. Many of my classmates and friends think of me as a person who has a great personality which makes it easy for me to work well with others. I have a very close bond with my friends and I would never take my friends for granted. My friends know that I have worked very hard to build these friendships and involvements. I am viewed as a good student. I am seen as contemplative, consistent, and intellectual. My teachers say that I always go full force until I have accomplished my goals. I am seen as determined, motivated, and extremely stubborn.

I was very flattered to hear all the positive feedback from friends and family. I agree with these positive comments but sometimes these traits can give me a rough time. For example, I can be very stubborn and opinionated to the point where I end up in conflicts with my friends or family members. Being opinionated helps me express myself and be my own person. In addition to the traits I have already listed, I also believe I am a person with very high morals. I value the fact that I am talkative and outgoing. These traits help me have close bonds with friends and family. Sometimes I perceive myself as being unsure. This is something I would like to change. I overreact sometimes which creates barriers that complicate my life.

I am satisfied with myself and my life. Of course there are things I want to change but overall I believe I have accomplished many goals and I have a lot to be proud of. I don't know exactly what

I am looking for but my theory is that if I keep pushing myself and accomplishing different goals, someday I will find out more about who I am and what I need to be happy. Right now it is difficult to even think about how I hope to be when I'm thirty years of age but I think I want to be married to a great, supporting, loving husband and have two beautiful children. I want a job that pays well and is rewarding. I am considering becoming a surgeon or working in the field of medical research. I want to live in a big farmhouse on a ranch with horses by the ocean. I am putting much effort into reaching my goals and I believe I am heading in the right direction.
    Rebecca, 1997

Eighteen

Time cannot break the bird's wing from the bird.
Bird and wing together
Go down, one feather.

No thing that ever flew,
Not the lark, not you,
Can die as others do.
　　　　Edna St. Vincent Millay, "To A Young Poet", Collected
　　　　Poems

Rage descends, its ugly dimensions far surpassing any anger I've
previously experienced...

I think about the others who perished that night. Like you, Tim died after being thrust from the cab of the truck. His cousin, Mike, was found unmoving in the front seat, still sitting next to where you had been only moments before. I see his face like that of a mannequin, his expression disbelieving, eyes wide open. One of the other boys walked away from the accident with only minor injuries. Another was hospitalized for a short time with minimal internal injuries.

And Tommie, he was in the hospital for well over a month, close to death on more than one occasion. The physical injuries he sustained can't even begin to compare to the emotional pain he will have to endure for the rest of his life. I think about him surviving the crash with a body that is torn and broken. I wonder how he is going to cope with the knowledge that he took your life and those of the two other boys. I would not want to live with that reality. My thoughts go to his parents. How awful it must be for them to witness Tommie's emotional and physical pain. They, too, must be in the midst of a terrifying nightmare.

In those first weeks after the accident, I felt profound pity for Tommie. I hoped that he would find a way to rebuild his life. I knew he needed help to ensure that he would never again bring this devastation on another family. I imagined that rehab might help, but I also hoped that he would find a positive purpose for his life.

People ask me if I am angry. They want to prepare me for the rage that is sure to come, reminding me that it is one of the stages in the grieving process. The anger does not surface until I hear that Tommie is conscious and talking about the crash. Word travels fast in our community.

Tommie has been moved from County Hospital to UCLA. Word has it that he told someone he is doing "all right except for having killed his three best friends". His words strike me as cavalier and sarcastic. When Tommie is released home, I hear that he refers to that night as "just a bad accident". If only that were the case. The facts point to something far more pitiful and sorrowful than just a bad accident. Your death and that of the other two boys could have been prevented.

It is becoming increasingly clear that Tommie had a drinking problem. If he was under the influence at the time of the crash, then this was no accident. Tommie killed you and those two other young people. His behaviour was criminal. He had no business being behind the wheel that night. These deaths, *your death*, could have been avoided. I am devastated. How could he put you in this kind of jeopardy? He was supposed to be your friend, someone who cared about you, who took care of you. The fact that he worked mixing drinks in a local restaurant means that he had more knowledge than most people about the potency of the alcohol he consumed and the way it would impair his judgment and reflexes. It was part of his job to monitor how much others were drinking and to determine whether they had exceeded a safe limit. Ironic, isn't it? Something more to be angry about.

The police report has been released. It is now at the District Attorney's office and is going through yet another level of analysis to determine whether or not charges will be filed. The California Highway Patrol is recommending that Tommie be charged with Vehicular Manslaughter While Intoxicated, Driving Under the Influence Causing Death, and three enhancements, one for each of the victims. The report does not cite a blood alcohol level. It is up to the District Attorney to decide whether or not that will be released. Still, it is obvious that Tommie was drinking and driving that night.

I hunger to know as much about the accident and the investigation as possible and so surround myself with the gory details, the numbers, the calculations. Rage descends, its ugly dimensions far surpassing any anger I have previously experienced. I feel it in the pit of my stomach. The rage consumes me. It seeps into my thoughts, my conversations, my dreams. I could drown in it. I picture myself being dragged down by an angry undertow, then struggling to reach the ocean's surface for air, only to be slammed back down and held under water. The next stage has begun.

*   *   *   *   *

I Do Not Understand...

I do not understand
why smart people don't try.
Why people hurt others to make
themselves feel good.
Why war is supposed to resolve
problems but really only makes
things worse.
But most of all
I do not understand why not all people teach
their children
to love and care for the world
and others.
We see many people hurting the world and
the creatures that
live in it.
What I understand most is
treating others with the same
kindness and respect I want them
to give me.
Why can't it be like this?
The world would be a better place.
    Rebecca, May 4, 1996

Nineteen

The most painful state of being is remembering the future,
particularly the one you'll never have.
  Søren Kierkegaard, Journalen

There's still the wanting, the wishing for what we can never have...

Perhaps there are always regrets. This is what has been on my mind today—the lost opportunities, the thoughts I can never share with you, the activities I believed we had more than enough time to get to. If you were here, you would try to reassure me. You would tell me not to worry and remind me that we had done so much already. You would say that we had done it all, if only in our minds.

Perhaps, but there is still the wanting, the wishing for what we can never have. I picture the way you might smile in acknowledgement at some of those lost opportunities. Other things we have lost, you might see as silly. You would most likely wonder why they even matter to me. But they do, Bec. *Everything* matters now.

I hear your words and feel you wrap your arms around me in a tight bear hug. "Ah, Mom," you say with a sigh. "Don't worry so much. You are so sad. I hate it when you're sad. Just enjoy everything that we had."

I try, and yet…

There was a morning not long before your death when you came downstairs and found Bob and me finishing breakfast and battling our way through a game of backgammon. You drifted by, commenting that you never could completely figure out the game. You made a fleeting remark about how you preferred Scrabble to backgammon. I was surprised and told you that I hadn't realized that you liked Scrabble.

"Of course, I do," you insisted. "Why do you think I always play when we're at Grandma's?"

"We'll have to play it more often then," I answered.

Bob asked if you wanted to join us for breakfast. But you were already headed for the door, intent on washing your car and going for a hike with friends. I made a mental note to invite you to play a game of Scrabble sometime soon. I figured that was something the three of us could do together. There was plenty of time for that. *Plenty of time.* How quickly it has disappeared.

Do you know what else I regret? I wish that we had gone to dinner again, just the two of us, no one else. I imagine us going downtown to your favorite Thai restaurant. We would order the spicy coconut soup with slices of ginger and mushrooms and chicken floating in the broth, a small Bunsen burner beneath the metal pot keeping the soup steaming hot. You were only twelve or thirteen the first time you had *Tom Kha Gai*. From then on, it was the one item on the menu that you routinely ordered when we went out for Thai food.

I don't know if you remember, but there was one evening years and years ago that I still often think about. Jake was at Aaron's for an overnight, and you and I were home alone. You had a sore throat and weren't quite yourself. We decided on takeout for dinner. We bundled up and drove downtown in search of your favorite soup. We talked easily while waiting for our order, then continued the conversation on the drive home and far into the evening. I don't remember what it was we spoke of, only that it was important to both of us. What I do recall is how lovely an evening it was. We ate steaming bowls of *Tom Kha Gai* and then snuggled together in my bed and watched a movie before dozing off. How I wish we had been able to have dinner together one more time, Becca, just the two of us.

I had told myself, "After the holidays, when life calms down a bit, Becky and I will have that special evening together."

Now, I wonder why I allowed myself to believe that there wasn't any rush or urgency. Why did I delude myself into thinking that we had all the time in the world?

Something else which I regret is that when you recently asked me to pull out my guitar and sing to you, I put you off, making an excuse about not being in the mood. I promised you that we would sing another day soon. I should have captured the moment and taken the opportunity when you offered it. I am so sorry for that, my darling girl. You told me that when you were small you loved to hear me sing to you. You asked why I didn't play much anymore and said you missed it. I explained about my wrist aching from carpal tunnel and that playing guitar aggravated it.

"Just play for a little while," you said.

"Not tonight. I'm tired, Bec. I will soon, though."

Oh, how I would welcome the discomfort in my arm for another opportunity to sing to you right now.

The year before you died, you asked me to organize our pictures into photo albums. Not just any albums, you wanted us to create scrapbooks with brightly colored, artsy borders and titles on each page. The task was daunting, but I reluctantly agreed. We shopped for the materials, scavenging through the local stores for the right papers and stickers. You were excited at the prospect of us working on this project together, but creating picture albums was never something I was much good at. Boxes upon boxes of photos from your childhood are proof of that. The early pictures are categorized by the year, with the photos segmented into plastic bags waiting for the right time to be placed in the albums.

As we began the task of assembling the scrapbooks, your excitement quickly gave way to frustration. Our progress was far slower than either of us had anticipated, and the resulting product was not quite as aesthetically pleasing as you had hoped. After a few attempts, we put the cardboard boxes back into a cupboard and promised one another we would return to the task at a later date. The boxes still remain in the family room cabinet. Now, I am faced with assembling the photos on my own. I mourn the fact that it is no longer something you and I can do together.

Regrets. Shortly after your death, Uncle Sid wrapped me in a fierce bear hug. "No regrets," he told me. "No regrets."

I knew he was referring to the recent death of his wife and the way he looked back at the life he and Toby had shared. How wonderful, I thought, to survive your spouse of fifty years and be able to say the two of you did it all, had time for everything you wanted.

But that is not us, my love. Your death came far too soon for that. Unlike Uncle Sid, I am haunted by questions of what could have been. I am not ready to let go, not ready to relinquish my plans and hopes. I am left with lingering regrets, with images of all that we will never have.

Bob and I take the dogs to the park. There, on the swings, are two small children. A young woman pushes one child, while an older woman tends to the other. A few feet away is a gray-haired man who watches the scene and smiles. The older couple must be grandparents and the young woman their daughter. I picture you. I will never be able to go to the park with you and your children. I will not have the opportunity to see you become a mother. *Endless regrets.*

*   *   *   *   *

My Future

It is both easy and hard to imagine what my life will be like when I am thirty years old. It is easy to imagine because I most likely will be dancing and have a family. It is also hard to imagine what kind of job I will have and where I will be living.

In the next few years I will be going to high school and college and studying ballet. I also plan to spend a lot of time with my friends. I am looking forward to high school. I am also sort of scared. I am not going to be with all my friends. We are going to be split up and that is the part I really hate. I went through that when I went from elementary school to middle school. It was hard at first but now I have a lot of great new friends. I also have my old ones.

I know that I am for sure going to go to college. I do not know what I want to study. Maybe I will study dance but I do not really have to worry about that yet because it is a long way off. I might be interested in being a professional dancer. I also like working with animals. I could be a veterinarian. I also have thought about being a teacher because lots of people say I am really good with children. Maybe I could combine teaching and dancing.

I hope to have a family. I also hope to have two kids, a boy and a girl. I want to have some animals but I do not have any idea what kind I want. I want to have a really big, fancy house. I also want to live somewhere else other than Ventura.

I think it is sort of interesting to think about how my life will be from now until I am thirty years old. Some of it is hard to imagine but some is really easy to imagine. I hope the things I want to have happen do come true. If I work very hard at it these can come true.

Rebecca, 1994

Twenty

Nothing is that can pause or stay;
The moon will wax, the moon will wane,
The mist and cloud will turn to rain,
The rain to mist and cloud again,
To-morrow be to-day.
      Henry Wadsworth Longfellow, "Kéramos", Kéramos and
      Other Poems

I drank in your features, studied the curves, the lines, the colors and
textures, everything about you...

I wish you joy and serenity, my girl. I wish you safety and a place to feel comfortable and at home. Most of all, I wish you a sense of belonging because that was always so much of a struggle for you.

There were times when you doubted our love, fearing that the bond that Dad and I had with you was less than our connection with Jacob. In your mind, the biological thread that ran between us and your brother somehow forged a deeper love than what we had with you. That was so far from the truth! I loved you from the very first moment I saw you,

Rebecca. You were every bit a part of me, as much as if you had grown in my womb like your brother. But you desperately wanted to have been born to Dad and me. You wanted to look like others in the family. You attributed some of your difficulties to not being our birth child.

School was often an issue for you. You were frustrated and angered as you watched Jacob cruise through class after class, racking up good grades without much effort. You, on the other hand, put in hours of studying. You fought for your grades and wrestled with a learning disability that you were sure was inherited from your biological parents.

You were so hurt by the fact that your biological mother had given you up. You saw her choice as a rejection rather than as the ultimate sacrifice. Intellectually, you knew she gave you up to a world of increased opportunities and a better life than she could have provided for you. Still, the fact that you were given up for adoption caused you tremendous pain. Of course, as your mother, I wanted to shield you from that pain. It hurt to watch you grapple with these issues, and it saddened me when I was unable to soothe your yearning for roots and identity.

*   *   *   *   *

The phone call announcing your birth came late in the evening. Dad and I were eager to adopt, but had prepared ourselves for a prolonged search. Instead, we were fortunate to find you after only one month's effort. We raced through the next couple of days, enlisting the help of family to prepare for your homecoming. Your father drove off to pick up a crib donated to us by a friend. When your Grandma Barbara heard that you were going to be sleeping in a hand-me-down crib, she was very upset, insisting that she would purchase a brand new one instead. But when she realized that the friend who was giving us the crib was a rabbi, the problem was solved.

The crib had been transformed from second-hand to a cherished item.

Others in the family went in search of diapers, bottles, and formula. Grandma and I descended on a local baby store and bought a mobile to hang above your crib, baby clothes, and an array of blankets. We weren't quite finished with our shopping when a call came into the store for us. It was your father announcing that he had heard from the attorney who was arranging the adoption and that we now had the go-ahead to drive the sixty miles north to the hospital in Port Hueneme where you were waiting for us. Grandma and I raced out of the store, arms laden with packages. I imagine the salespeople thought we were out of our minds when we told them that our baby had arrived and that we needed them to ring up our items as quickly as possible.

You were only two days old when your father and I went to get you.

"Your daughter is down there," an accommodating nurse told us, sending us through a medicinal-smelling maze.

Your daughter—no one had ever before said those words to me. They were the most beautiful words I had ever heard. My prayers for a child had finally been answered.

Further down the hallway, another nurse approached us and asked if we were the Beilins. You lay in her arms, a tiny bundle wrapped in a pink receiving blanket. "This is your daughter," the woman announced. Again, those amazing words.

As she handed you to me, I drank in your features, studied the curves, the lines, the colors and textures, everything about you. I thought that I would never be able to pull my gaze away from you. I memorized your tiny dollop of a nose, your dainty rose-colored lips, the generous topping of dark brown hair that framed your face. You were gorgeous, perfectly formed and so delicate, the most exquisite child I had ever seen. Your dark eyes were surrounded by long, thick lashes that fanned out like thin fronds.

"You'll want to change her in there." The nurse pointed to a small room nearby. "You can dress her in her clothes and wrap her up in a blanket. Tell us when you're finished, and we'll take care of all the paperwork."

Your father and I stared at one another. He was the first to speak. "How do we dress her?" he stammered. "Can we bend her arms and legs without breaking them?"

The nurse laughed. "Gently bend her limbs. You'll do fine. You won't hurt her."

Given our lack of experience, the woman's words did little to reassure us. Still, we followed her instructions and tackled our first task as parents. We maneuvered you into a dressing gown, taking far more care than was needed in slipping your arms into the sleeves and sliding the rest of you into the soft cotton fabric. We placed tiny booties on your feet and wrapped you up in one of the flannel blankets that Grandma and I had bought earlier that day. You didn't seem at all disturbed by the process.

Walking out of the hospital with you, I thought: *This is my baby, my child.* I touched your cheek, amazed by the silky softness of your skin and the way your mouth puckered a bit at the sensation.

We were told that your birth mother had left the hospital just about the time that we were arriving. While we never had the opportunity to meet her, we apparently passed her in the hallway on our way in. I have a vague memory of a woman who looked away as we approached. She was short in stature, with straight brown hair that reached below her shoulders. She seemed sad as she left. At the time, I had no way of knowing she was your birth mother.

I can only guess that leaving that hospital without you was the most difficult thing she had ever done in her life. I will always be grateful to her for entrusting you to us. I hope she understands what a precious gift she gave us and how we accepted that trust and responsibility with solemn and heartfelt intentions.

From that day forward, you have been my daughter, Rebecca. I often think that it was fate that brought us together. Families come into being in different ways. You, your father, and I happened to become a family through adoption. Strange as it may sound, finding you made me thankful that I had been unable to conceive. It allowed me to have you in my life.

How many times since your death have I replayed that first day of our becoming a family? I think about the tiny, vulnerable infant who was entrusted into my care. How desperately I want to go back to that day. It was so much easier to keep you safe when you were small.

Soon after your birth, one of Grandma's friends told me that this was a time to cherish, that it was the most uncomplicated time in child-rearing. Grace said that as the years went by, parenting would become more complicated. I wondered how that could be.

As an infant, you were often awake during the night, needing to be fed and held, wanting to be rocked and cuddled until you finally fell back to sleep. You were the same way during the day, content if we were holding you, but protesting loudly whenever we set you down. As much as I adored you, I was exhausted by the demands of parenting. This was all so new to me. It was draining to be needed constantly, to have someone so little calling the shots.

As the years passed, I came to understand what Grace had meant about your first year of life being the simplest and easiest time. Back then, your needs were specific, and I was able to meet them. I was able to protect you. There were obvious things that needed to be done in order to keep you healthy and safe.

As you matured and became more independent, parenting became more complicated. There had to be a balance between keeping you safe and allowing you to grow and mature. By the time you were a teenager, life was even more challenging. You had a loud and sometimes strident voice and definite opinions about almost everything. Decisions had to be weighed and navigated through. I was able to keep you safe when you were small, but not when you were older. I could caution you and direct you, but in the end, your decisions belonged to you. We all have to endure the terrible consequence.

*   *   *   *   *

My Name

The formal version of my name is Rebecca Amy Singer-Beilin. The informal version of my name is Becca Amy Singer-Beilin. I was named after my great-grandma, Sylvie, and my great-grandpa, Albert. My great-great grandmother was also named Rebecca. My middle name, Amy, has significance because it starts with the same letter as my great-grandfather's name, Albert. It is a Jewish tradition to name a child with the same first initial as a deceased relative's name.

My parents named me but we had a rabbi named David Berner do the naming ceremony. Lots of family were there. It was a very important time for the family. The rabbi said a blessing for me and then we had a special party.

If I were the opposite sex I would have been named David Michael. I am so glad I wasn't the opposite sex because I really like myself. I like the name David Michael, but I am glad I am a girl.

In Hebrew, Rebecca means to tie or braid. It also means beautiful in Hebrew. My name comes from the Torah. My Hebrew name is Hannah Sarah, but a direct translation would be Rebecca Hannah. You can have a Hebrew name that does not exactly match your English name. I really like my name. I also think I look like a Rebecca. Some of my nicknames are Bec-a-boo, Bec, Becky, and Becca. I really like all my nicknames, but I like Becca the best. Becca is my favorite nickname because it is what I am used to being called.

I don't really know what I want to name my children. I really have not given it much thought. I do not have to think about it now because I have a long time to worry about that. I won't have children for a very long time.

I am glad my name is Rebecca. Even though I have never really thought about it before, it would be hard to imagine being named something other than Rebecca. I grew up with the name Rebecca and that's what I'm used to. I like the name Rebecca Amy Singer-Beilin.

Rebecca, 1993

Twenty One

Hope is the thing with feathers that perches in the soul — and sings the tunes without the words — and never stops at all.
Emily Dickinson, The Complete Poems of Emily Dickinson

So many things I wished for you, so many things you wished for yourself...

Death took you far too soon. There was so much of life ahead of you. I wish that you had lived long enough to find your soul mate. Remember the conversations we had about what it would be like when you met someone with whom you could feel safe? You deserved to be with a man who would cherish you, who would be worthy of all the love and passion you had to offer. I relaxed a bit when you told me that you weren't sure that David was the one you would marry. I had seen that relationship as tumultuous. It didn't seem to satisfy your need to belong and to feel protected.

You so desperately wanted safety and security in a relationship. That was something that would have come later, after you had matured. But first, you had to reach a point of feeling at ease with yourself. Like most parents, I wanted that for you.

It was not long after you and David had parted ways that you and I stayed up late to talk. You told me about the boys you had dated. You even broached the subject of sex and the mixture of feelings that accompanied it. You trusted me enough to say that you didn't enjoy sex all that much but liked the bonding it provided. At the time, I was struck by your choice of words and wondered if that was the aftermath of having two parents and a stepfather who were therapists. I told you about my own self-consciousness and insecurities in my relationship with your father and how fortunate I was to have married my best friend the second time around. You gently touched the sapphire ring Bob had given me for my fiftieth birthday and said that you hoped you would end up with someone who would love you enough to give you such a beautiful gift.

"You will," I promised. "Give yourself a chance."

"I thought I'd have that with David," you said. "I guess I was wrong about that."

I reminded you how young you and David were when you started dating and suggested that it would be a good idea for you to be on your own for a while, to get comfortable with yourself before getting involved in another relationship. You said that you hated being alone but knew it was what you needed to do. Then you asked how you would know when you met the right person.

I said something about being able to be yourself without pretense and feeling safe and comfortable. You nodded in agreement and observed that Bob goes shopping with me and doesn't mind doing what you called *girl stuff*. When you indicated that you wanted a guy who would do that with you, I told you to figure that into the equation, to consider what you wanted from a relationship and what qualities someone would have to have in order to meet your expectations.

"I don't want to get married until I'm at least thirty," you announced. "I don't want to rush into things and end up getting divorced the way Dad and you did." You went on to say that it would take a long time to figure out who you were and what you wanted in a relationship.

"That's a good plan," I agreed.

You curled against me and fell asleep in my arms, my girl-child who was growing into such an amazing woman.

*   *   *   *   *

Your death has silenced so many dreams, all the hopes I had for your future. What is left are remnants of your life. Sometimes I think of these dreams as being tangible. I picture them floating about in the universe, searching for you. I like to think that wherever you are right now, that you are substituting new dreams for the old ones, different hopes for a future that exists in a realm that I can only imagine.

You and I were so full of words. We talked; we wrote things down. Our thoughts and feelings swirled around the house and filled up the space. I sift through your writings and find bittersweet comfort. All the things you wanted to do in your lifetime, Becca! I read your poems and essays again and again and cherish the memories. So many things I wished for you, so many things you wished for yourself.

*   *   *   *   *

I have very mixed feelings about the topic of marriage. I know that marriage is not something crucial for me to think about right now. I am an eighteen-year-old college student. I have a boyfriend, but have no immediate plans to get married. I expect to think about this more in the future because I will want to get married at some point in my life. Marriage is not one of my priorities right now; eventually it will be. Hopefully, after I have a stable career and have gotten the chance to have more life experiences, I will consider marriage.

Too many people are getting divorced and there is no point in getting married to get divorced. In many ways though I do want to get married but I am scared that it won't work. I want to get married because I want to have someone to share my life with. I want children and a husband. I think it is very important for children to have both a father and a mother. I would not want to deprive my children of this. I want to have someone who loves me unconditionally and I him.

One of my worries is that I don't want to get hurt. This has repeatedly happened to me and I do not want to go through it again. Connected to this worry is the concern that I would not want to love a person and then either get divorced or have him die. I do not want to put myself in a position where I can experience a great loss.

Right now I am in a relationship which I want to continue for a long period of time. When I talked with my boyfriend, David, about wanting a long-term relationship, he voiced ambivalence. At this point in his life, he cannot think in terms of continuing our relationship long term; he is very involved in his career. In turn, I was very hurt by his reluctance to commit to continuing our relationship. This goes back to me not wanting to get married or seriously involved because of the fear of getting hurt

The whole topic of marriage can bring up very painful memories. I come from a divorced family. My parents got divorced when I was about eleven years old. This really affected my life, and in many ways it still does. I could not understand how my parents stopped loving each other. I wanted them to be back together. I wanted us—my brother, myself and our parents—to be a family again. My grandma used to tell me if I wanted something really bad I could wish for it and eventually it would come true. Every night after their divorce I would wish for us to be a family again. No matter how much I wished, this dream would never come true.

I am too young to be considering marriage. I have many other topics that I need to focus on instead of marriage. For example, school is very important to me and my focus should be there. I also need to *think about school next year. I need to decide if I will stay at Ventura College or if I will go away to a university or a state school. I am in need of a job and I need to put a great deal of energy into finding one because it is time consuming. Finding a car is also another pressing issue. I don't have a reliable means of transportation so I need to look for a more efficient car. All of these topics are more important to me than considering marriage. I would rather be more committed to dealing with these.*

Many young adults in my generation do not seem to take marriage very seriously. Our lives seem to be too busy to involve considering marriage. We have many other issues to deal with. We are engulfed in living our lives as prosperously as we can day by day, not worrying about the future. Marriage is a lifetime commitment, and most young adults are too preoccupied with their present lives to have time for a lifetime commitment.

Getting married can be an amazing experience. There are changes that marriage can make in an individual. One major thing that can happen is a loss of identity. A person can start to refer to themselves as "us" or "we" instead of "I" or "me". It can become difficult to be oneself and still be part of a couple. It might be very useful for each partner to maintain some separate interests and friends. Furthermore, it is crucial that each partner remain aware of their own feelings and thoughts and true to her/himself.

I have many mixed feelings dealing with the topic of marriage. This has been reflected throughout my essay. I have many hopes and dreams about marriage and I have some positive expectations for the future. However, writing this essay has been very difficult for me. I find this topic extremely strenuous to write about given my age and pressing issues. I spend a great deal of time trying to push the topic of marriage out of my head. It just seems to create an unnecessary distraction for me. I should be focusing on getting my life in order and getting an education so that I can have a career. This all must happen before I can consider marriage.

Rebecca, 1998

Twenty Two

For after all, the best thing one can do
When it is raining, is to let it rain.
    Henry Wadsworth Longfellow, "The Poet's Tale", Tales of a
    Wayside Inn

Promises of rain...

The sky is pregnant with dark clouds and promises of rain. Bob and I bundle up and walk to the gym, determined to get in some exercise before tackling the obligations of the day. As I begin my workout, the pattering of water against the skylight draws my attention upward. Within minutes, it is pouring. Bob and I are sure to be soaked on our walk home. I don't mind. In fact, I rather like the idea.

Once outside, I let the rain wash over my hair and face. It rejuvenates me, cleanses me. Bob pulls his sweatshirt up to cover his neck and head. I laugh at the awkward sight. We arrive home to dogs who are wet and muddy. They find sanctuary in the garage. Bob disappears to take the first shower while I dry Rocky and Zoey. I discard dripping shoes and socks and then go in search of a warm shower.

It rains throughout the day. At times, the rain is so gentle that the droplets of water seem suspended in air. Other times, the rain descends in strong, angry torrents.

You were impervious to the rain. It never stopped you from any activity. Today, the rain unleashes powerful images of you—the sound of your laughter, your eyes sparkling in anticipation as you head out to play in the rain, and the smell of your wet hair. Today there is much to be grateful for. I have you close at hand. *Write down these images,* I tell myself. *Make sure you preserve their substance and soul.*

*   *   *   *   *

Promises of rain. A downpour would not deter you. Instead, it brightened your twelve-year-old face, filling it with eagerness and excitement. The sheet of water was the perfect backdrop for your activities. While many children saw a rainy day as confining and a source of irritation, you viewed it as an opportunity for exploration and adventure. Think of it! Water gushing down the street forming a veritable stream only feet from our house! Dirt turning to wet, gooey mud—the perfect medium for creating mud pies or sculpting wild creations. And when the rain began to lift, there was always the hope of a rainbow arching its way across the brightening sky in a band of brilliant color.

On this particular day, the downpour was fortuitous. You had a captive audience in your brother and three of your cousins. They were content to participate in any activity you organized. The five of you donned boots and jackets before venturing forth into the elements. I watched from inside as you led the younger children across the rain-soaked lawn to the curb where water was already cascading down from the nearby foothills. You were the pied piper and your brother and cousins your jubilant followers. You leaped off the curb into the swirling stream, gleeful at the huge splash. Of course, the other kids followed suit. All of you marched up and down the street, smiling faces turned up toward the rain.

Knowing that all of you would eventually need something to ease the chill, I put a pot of mulled cider on the stove to heat. An hour later, the five of you showed up on the doorstep, soaked through and through. You stripped out of your soggy clothes into sweats and pajamas and settled at the dining room table where I delivered the mugs of steaming cider. The five of you were full of stories about your adventures in the rain.

*   *   *   *   *

It has continued to rain through most of the week. Sunday night finds us with family. Marggie and Linda have joined us for dinner, along with Linda's brother, someone I have not seen in well over thirty-five years.

As soon as dinner is over, your cousins dodge the adult conversation and venture into the wet night. I wander from the table to watch the kids play in the rain. The way they stomp through the puddles unearths memories from years ago. When your cousins come back inside, they are drenched, their faces full of smiles. No one mentions the fact that you are not here or that you were the one who used to orchestrate these escapades. You have taught them well, Rebecca. Your cousins have not forgotten how to play in the rain.

The evening is filled with good conversation and more laughter than has been heard in this house in a very long time. Even so, it all seems so very fragile. Everyone avoids talking about you. Your cousins shy away from saying your name. Alan does not ask about you or your brother, a startling omission given all of the catching up we have been doing. At one point in the evening, I try to steer the conversation to you and Jake, but others take the conversation in different directions. Do they really think that not talking about you will keep me from remembering, from missing you? Don't they realize that you are a constant presence? Their silence does nothing to ease my grief. *Say her name,* I want to tell them. *Fill me with stories and memories of Becky.* Tonight, I will have to be content with my own private images of you.

Once our guests leave, I head upstairs to get ready for bed. I stare out at at the dark night and listen to the rain. You are everywhere, Becca. The rain has brought me the gift of memories. Rain is something to be celebrated.

*   *   *   *   *

Last night it rained and rained and today it will rain a lot. I love it when it rains because of the earth needing water and because of the nice earthy smell. It is nice but the only thing I don't like about the rain is that it gets inside the car and we get all wet but it is all right.

Rebecca, February 3, 1992

Twenty Three

To weep is to make less the depth of grief.
    William Shakespeare, Henry VI

I begin to think of my grief as something fluid...

Bob's knee is sore. Having decided to give it a few days rest, he opts out of our early morning walk, leaving me to set off on my own.

I catch sight of a young woman who is sitting in a car on the far side of the intersection. Her hair is the same color and length as yours, even parted down the middle the way you used to wear yours. Her face is familiar—round, with cheek bones set high, a small upturned nose, and large eyes lengthened into soft ellipses. Even the way she turns her head from side to side as she waits for an opening in traffic reminds me of you.

For a long moment, I am convinced that this woman is you. And I think, perhaps you didn't die after all. It is possible, isn't it? I reason that you got upset and took off without telling me. All this time, you've been living close by and we didn't know it. I continue on with the scenario, proposing that when you heard that we thought you were dead, you were too embarrassed or afraid to call, so you stayed away. I desperately want these things to be true. Then you would be able to come home to us. The tragedy of Thanksgiving morning could disappear, perhaps be some horrific nightmare and not reality at all. Imagine, you would still be alive! God, how I want that to be so.

The truth is, though, that these are only a mother's hopeless dreams. They have no substance, no grounding in reality. Everyone in my world knows that you died on Thanksgiving morning. If all of them believe that to be true, how can it be any other way?

When we first got the news about the crash, Bob insisted on going to the mortuary to say goodbye to you. He knew I would hold fast to doubts that you had died. He understood how crucial it would be for him to be able to dissuade me from my fantasies. He had to be able to tell me that it was really you who was lying lifeless in that pine coffin. He had to be able to tell me without question, without hesitation, that you had died.

As the traffic light changes, I wonder if any of the passersby have noticed my anguish. I don't care. My pain is not something to be hidden away. It is part of who I am. *Reanne Singer, Mother of the Young Woman Who Died*—that is who I have become. No longer psychologist, friend, writer. Instead, I am the woman who has to live with the tragedy of losing her daughter.

The phone calls and condolence cards have slowed. The shock of your death is waning, and in its stead comes a hollow, aching pain. Having weathered the loss of his mother, Bob tells me that the sorrow does not go away. It is tenacious and permanent. He uses the analogy of walking along the ocean's edge when the water is calm and the tide line easily negotiated. But all that can change without much warning as the water sweeps further up on the shore. That is when you find yourself scurrying away with the waves chasing at your heels. As quickly as the water has pushed its way up the sand, it recedes once again, leaving the tide line as it was before. This, Bob says, is the way grief and sorrow work. It lulls the mourner into complacency, into believing that life is returning to normal. And then it hits. It pounds against you and reminds you once again of your loss. Bob assures me that the time will come when I will ride these waves of sorrow with greater ease.

I begin to think of my grief as something fluid, as something that changes form and dimension. It is no less powerful than it was in the beginning. The transformation is in realizing that there will be calm after the overwhelming waves of sorrow. I have the capacity to make it through each rise and fall of emotion, each rise and fall of the tides of grief. I have done it a million times already.

*   *   *   *   *

A four-day weekend looms before us. Bob and I threaten to go camping, but then talk ourselves out of it. I suggest that we remain in town and go on day trips, perhaps to Los Angeles or Santa Barbara. The weekend evaporates without us going anywhere. Friday, I work on my novel. Bob and I spend Saturday and Sunday cleaning out the office, doing yard work, and straightening up around the house. Monday morning again finds us entertaining the possibility of an outing, but by this point, neither one of us is very motivated. We're both in strange moods, fidgety and unsettled. At my suggestion, we decide to visit the cemetery. This will be my first time there since your funeral six weeks ago.

We take with us things we think you would like—shells, ocean glass, flowers from our garden. We drive through the entrance of the cemetery. The tall wrought iron gates stand sentry. Jewish tradition has us wait one year before placing the headstone, so your grave remains unmarked. Since you are buried near an old family friend, I use her grave as a guide to find yours. Bob loosens the metal flower container from the dirt at the head of your grave and goes in search of water. Sitting down on the grass, I run my fingers through the green blades. Sadness swells in the small of my throat, its physical presence a hard ball that threatens to cut off my air. I choke out a few words and tell you about the things we have brought for you. I arrange the shells and ocean glass on top of your grave. My breathing is jerky and uneven. I struggle for air.

"I miss you," I whisper. "I love you, Becca."

My cheeks are wet, my mouth filled with the taste of salt. I flash on a memory of swimming with you in the ocean, the tangy saltwater filling my mouth as I am pushed under by a wave. And then the current bounces me up to the surface where I see you splashing, laughing—my child who was every bit as comfortable in the water as you were on land.

"I want you to be at peace, my love. I want you to experience joy and to take care of yourself."

As my crying eases, I notice other pieces of ocean glass on your grave. I touch each bit of glass and wonder who has brought these here. Perhaps Grandma Barbara and Aunt Leslie. As my hand again settles in the grass, I think about the way your hand used to feel in mine—small, firm, strong. I think about brushing your hair, the long silky strands gliding through my fingers, each lock glistening as it captured the sunlight.

Bob returns with the water-filled container. I set the flowers in it. When he tries to adjust the arrangement, I stop him and put the flowers back the way I had them, intent on leaving as much of me in this place with you as I can.

Bob asks if I am going to talk to you. I respond with a self-conscious shrug.

"Well, Becky," he says, looking down at your grave, "I'm trying, but your mom doesn't talk to my mother either."

That's when I blurt out that I have already talked with you.

"Good," he says, smiling at me. He continues on, telling you that we love you and miss you and that he hopes you are doing okay. Like me, he asks that you take care of yourself, assures you that we are taking care of each other and trying to cope with your death. He places a pine cone on your grave as a marker that people who love you have been here and remembered you.

Before leaving the cemetery, we wash our hands at the outdoor fountain, following the Jewish custom of not bringing death back into the world with us. Some would say that this is a *bubbe meise,* an old grandmother's tale. Perhaps it is, but the superstitions that connected my grandmother to the Russian *shtetl* of her youth have their own power for me. I wash my hands out of habit, out of respect for tradition, and yes, out of fear of bringing more death into the world. I know, too, that this custom signifies a ritualistic transition from death back to life. In Torah, water is the source of life.

As we get in the car, I announce that I want to visit the crash site—another first. We drive the ten miles to the place of your death. Once there, I make my way to the edge of the road and stare over the embankment at the gully that not so very long ago held your lifeless body. Silence surrounds me. Without meaning to, I hold my breath.

This is where it happened. This is where my baby was killed.

If water is symbolic of life and transition, then it is important to acknowledge that this ravine is without water. It is dry and parched. This is where life was ripped away from your body. This is a place of violence, of sadness. Searching for some remnant of you, I scan the rocky terrain. There is no peace to be found here, only a deep embankment with a harsh outcropping of boulders that once cradled your broken body.

People have left memorials here for you and the two boys who perished along with you. A hand painted sign reads: *Staircase to Heaven* and another: *Tim, Mike, and Becky—Until we meet again...may God hold you in the palm of His hands.* There is a crudely carved cross and beneath that a hand-made Star of David. Someone has placed a beer bottle at the site; perhaps it is meant to be a reminder for others not to drink and drive. Disturbed by its presence, I hurl it as far away as I can before closing my eyes and whispering a prayer for you.

I pull myself away and remember that you are not here. Me leaving does not translate into abandoning you. Bob and I head home, having taken huge steps today in coping with your death.

*   *   *   *   *

Once I was
The first line of a letter
Undefined and plain
Now I am
A completed page
Yet to be written
Partially created
But not yet finished.
        Rebecca, 1995

Twenty Four

The soul of man is larger than the sky,
Deeper than the ocean, or the abysmal dark
Of the unfathomed center.
    David Hartley Coleridge, "To Shakespeare"

I find you everywhere in this place...

I have been completely overwhelmed with sadness over the last two weeks. My body is heavy, weighted down with all the sorrow. I plod through each day's tasks, but I'm detached, doing what I imagine is expected of me, what I expect of myself. I look in the mirror and study my own reflection, startled by the aging woman who seems so sad and worn. It is difficult for me to settle for any length of time. I'm uncomfortable outside the house and ill at ease at home. I roam from room to room in search of a place to light. I am restless and agitated, edgy in my own skin.

Is it possible for anyone else in the world to understand the depth of my sorrow? Your death is a continual presence for me that fills my waking hours as well as my dreams. Tears flow from my eyes like pus oozing from an inflamed sore. I cry so often that my eyes are habitually red and swollen.

A few weeks ago, I had a fleeting hope that life might soon become easier. Like someone who has been held under water and is desperate for a breath, I looked forward to surfacing for air. Even though you were always on my mind, I was coping a bit better. There was less trauma and struggle in my days. The strong waves of grief that had been tearing away at me were hitting less often. I even thought that I was becoming more able to contain those waves and save them for private moments when I was better prepared to deal with them. The sadness seemed less consuming than it had been, but the reprieve was short-lived.

The grief returns, every bit as brutal and unrelenting as it has ever been. Exhausted, I beg God to end this nightmare. I imagine that if I can find the right words, if I pray often enough and with sufficient passion, that God will bring you back to me. My prayers remain unanswered.

When I am at home, I find you everywhere in this place. Each room, every corner of this house, holds your memories. Your voice fills the dark rooms; your laughter beckons to me, summoning me up the stairs to search for you. And then I hear you calling to me.

"Mom..." I startle at the sound and struggle to reconcile it with my awareness that you have died.

Standing in your room, I stare at the framed photographs that adorn your shelves. I run a finger over your image and caress the contours of your face, your hair. I want more than this visual replica of you. I curl up on your bed and clutch your pillow in one hand and your picture in the other. Why won't you come home to me, Rebecca? Don't you understand that I need you here with me?

Bob arrives home earlier than expected. When he calls from downstairs, my answer is soft and shaky. He calls again and then tromps up the stairs, questioning out loud why the house is so dark. He switches on the hall light and spots me huddled in your room—eyes puffy and red, face mottled. He asks me what is wrong, but doesn't wait for my answer. He already knows.

"Rebecca," he whispers, and pulls me close.

*   *   *   *   *

At my invitation, your cousins sort through your clothing, taking sweaters and T-shirts home with them. I bundle up in a fleece jacket that still carries your scent and stumble on an unexpected treasure, your cinnamon colored hairs that cling to the fabric. Amazing! You have died, but I still have bits of your hair here with me.

Your father calls and asks if it would be all right for him and your stepmother to look through your belongings. We set a time. When they arrive, I am struck by the changes in your dad. He looks tired and so much older than before. His ashen complexion accentuates the dark circles beneath his eyes. His features are stiff and drawn tight. His expression reminds me of my own; he is filled with sadness. We both look like ghosts, like people who have outlived our allotted years.

Your father tells me that in recent weeks he has consulted with a psychic. I find this odd since he has always been such a skeptic, but I suppose your death has moved him to search for answers and consolation in unusual places. That the recommendation to this psychic came from your uncle makes her credibility suspect, but I keep my misgivings to myself and listen to what your father has to say, knowing that he is speaking from the heart.

According to the psychic, you did not suffer in the crash. She told your father that you died quickly and had an easy time crossing over to the Other Side. I hope this is true, but wonder if this isn't what most psychics would say.

She told your dad that you are now with his father, Grandpa Irwin, and his father as well. While I can picture you with Grandpa Irwin, I can't understand why you would be with your great-grandfather, someone who abandoned his family when Grandpa Irwin was a young boy. I don't imagine that you or your grandfather would find any comfort with this man.

The details of the reading become more disturbing when your father tells me that you are also with your biological mother. My stomach seizes. The only words I am able to choke out are to ask whether your dad knows if she has actually died. I want to prove him wrong. I want to tell him that she gave you up, gave you to me. I want to scream: *She's not Becca's mother! I am!* The depth of my rage and jealousy frightens me.

Your stepmother's voice calls me back. She reports hearing you when she's driving the school bus past the cemetery. She says that you talk to her and that she knows you're all right. I tell your father and Cathy that I often feel your presence. I mention about Bob and me hearing your footsteps in the house. Dad and I find some common ground in our grief.

I lead the way up to your room. Feeling the need to be present, I perch on your bed as your father and Cathy go through your things. I have to safeguard the process, make sure that all this is done in a sacrosanct way. My presence is unnecessary. Dad and Cathy are tender and respectful as they search for keepsakes for your stepsiblings. They repeatedly ask if I am comfortable with what they want to take. Cathy handles your clothing with care, folding it in neat piles and readying it for the next part of this journey.

They are at the house for over an hour. After I escort them out, I return to your room and sit for a long time in the quiet silence. I know you are here with me helping me through this. I feel your presence.

*   *   *   *   *

141

Reanne Singer

Finding Out Who I Am

Finding out who I am
Searching, curious, an unfinished journey
Feeling stuck and confused.
Persistent, the need to keep going
Clues discovered.
Honest, always striving for more.
Active, sometimes impatient,
Frustrated, struggling but getting nowhere,
Slowly making progress.
Feeling lost.

Through the years, losing innocence
Part of growing up,
Not sure if I like it.
Wanting to explore,
Finding new things,
Getting scared, running back home.

Family.
Supportive, loving.
Comfort,
Safety.
A shoulder to cry on.

Rebecca, December 9, 1996

Twenty Five

There is a sacredness in tears. They are not the mark of weakness, but of power. They speak more eloquently than ten thousand tongues. They are the messengers of overwhelming grief, of deep contrition, and of unspeakable love.
    Washington Irving

I weave my fingers through the blades of grass and cling to them as though they are a part of you...

The day is warm. Clouds trail overhead — spun silk against blue sky. As I drive through town to the cemetery, it occurs to me that there was a time when such a day would have made me happy, but not now, not as I take on the cemetery all by myself. I am anxious and unsure of myself, questioning whether I am actually ready to confront this place on my own.

Once inside the grounds, I cruise past a funeral party. The somber cast keeps vigil at an open grave. Memories of your funeral descend — walking into the sanctuary and standing before your coffin, fragile and light-headed as I stumble through the *Kaddish* prayer, poised at your burial site between Bob and Kevin and the awful sound of metal grinding against metal as your casket is lowered into the ground.

I climb out of the car. My eyes sting; a lump rises in my throat. The breeze is cool against my face and arms that are now damp with perspiration. I retrieve the flowers I have brought from home and free them from their wrapping of wet paper towels. *One foot in front of the other. One step at a time. That's all you have to do,* I tell myself. The wind rustles through the nearby trees. I look around to see if anyone else is here, but there is no one. *It is better to be by myself,* I think.

I make my way to where you are buried. Fresh flowers stand at the head of your grave. There's a note secured in place beneath the pine cone that Bob left for you the last time he was here. Bending down, I read the handwritten words: *I'll love you always.* The writing is not Bob's. Who has left this for you?

After filling the metal container with fresh water, I add my flowers to the others. Sitting next to your grave, I find myself wishing that your headstone was already in place. If something were to happen to Dad or me, who would make sure to mark your grave in our stead—Bob, Grandma, Grandpa, my sisters? Would any of them know the right words to have etched in the stone?

"I love you," I whisper. "I miss you," and then tell you that it is too hard having you gone like this and that I want you back here with me.

I weave my fingers through the blades of grass and cling to them as though they are a part of you. I think about the sound of your footsteps and the way it feels to lie quiet at night and feel you in my arms, against my chest.

"I want you to be safe and peaceful," I say, looking up at the sky now. I so much prefer thinking of you up in the heavens rather than down here buried deep in the ground. "I want you to take care of yourself and move forward on your journey. You don't have to stay here and take care of me, Becca. I don't want to stop you from moving on." When I add that you'll always be my girl, I wonder if this reassurance is more for your benefit or mine.

After raising my fingers to my lips, I trail a kiss down to your grave. "We've both been blessed. I love you."

Pulling myself to my feet, I walk past friends' graves. I ask Kathleen and Beverly to watch over you, then return to your grave and murmur a goodbye.

As I drive from the cemetery, I notice that the sky is dotted with clouds. *Think of her up there*, I tell myself. *Think of her up in the heavens.* Is this to be my new mantra? Maybe this is why I have made the trip alone today, to find some inner strength, another lifeline to keep me afloat.

*   *   *   *   *

Aqua

Aqua is as blue as the sky.
Aqua is as beautiful as a ring.
Aqua is as cold as ice.
Aqua is as wet as the sea.
Aqua is bright and alive.
Aqua is as exciting as a roller coaster.
Aqua is as colorful as the world.
Aqua is as sparkling as a tropical ocean.
Aqua is as tasty as a wintergreen mint.
Aqua is as innocent as a new baby.
Aqua is as smooth as a crystal.
Aqua is as shiny as a polished stone.
Aqua is as quiet as the soft wind.
Aqua is as scary as ocean's waves.
Aqua is as sweet as love

Rebecca, October 11, 1993

Twenty Six

We are ever dying to one world and being born into another.
Henry David Thoreau, Journal

People appear in my life for a reason...

There is meaning to be found in things that might previously have gone unnoticed. Conversations and interactions with others no longer seem as haphazard as they once did. I am convinced that people appear in my life for a reason, offering me parts of themselves that help me along this agonizing path. Your death does not serve some greater purpose, nor was it preordained. But I do know that there is a power far greater than you or me. Given that, I have to wonder whether the appearance of these people is God's doing. The only answer I can come to is perhaps.

Some people offer gifts of understanding and support. Others challenge my way of thinking; they urge me beyond the expected to new ways of understanding. The presence of these people is far more than happenstance. The synchronicity is at times astounding.

*   *   *   *   *

A phone call from my dentist twists in an unexpected direction. Sally asks how I am. When I share having sensed you nearby, she suggests that I talk with her assistant, who has had a longtime interest in life after death. Though I welcome Sally's invitation, it would not have occurred to me to talk with Karen about these things.

Still disturbed by the thought of you being with your birth mother, I search out information. I go online, but there is no trace of your birth mother there—not in the obituaries, the local paper, or news reports from the surrounding communities. I expand my search, looking for something, anything, to tell me whether she is alive or dead. Still nothing.

Monday finds me irritable and restless. Having overslept, I forfeit my workout at the gym in order to make it to the office on time. I watch the clock during the day, impatient for work to end. At five o'clock, I pack up my briefcase, intent on going to the gym before heading for home.

After a quick change in the dressing room, I snag the last available elliptical trainer. My strides are even and fast-paced, my breathing hard, but there is relief in the workout. Forty-five minutes later, I am in a better mood. Spotting Karen a few yards away, I go over to talk to her.

When she asks how I am doing, I shrug and tell her that I am up and down. She waits for me to say something more. I explain about the conversation with Sally and ask Karen if she would be willing to talk with me about death. She readily agrees. We arrange to meet at the dental office, choreographing a time when there are no patients.

When I arrive, Karen is seated behind the counter. She motions me to a nearby chair and explains that she is the only one there. As I take a seat, I wonder what I am supposed to say. Suddenly, the words pour out. I talk with Karen about you and me, our relationship. I describe what life has been like since your death.

"I feel Becky with me," I say, "at the house, when I'm out

walking, different places. I hear her footsteps. I hear her voice sometimes."

"Rebecca is always with you." Karen's voice is calm and even. "Sometimes you get calls and no one is on the other end of the phone."

My heart is pounding. My upper lip is damp with sweat. How can she possibly know about this? "Becca used to call me all the time," I confide. "Sometimes she wouldn't leave a message. When I would check the answering machine, there would be a hang-up call. I'd always know it was her and would immediately call her back."

Karen smiles, appearing not at all surprised.

"I'm getting tons of those calls now," I continue. "Multiple ones every day." My breathing is shallow. I rush to get the words out. "Becky and my mother were notorious for not leaving messages. Since Bec's death, I've asked my mother to leave a message when she calls; it's too upsetting to get the hang-up calls. But they're still happening; my mother promises that it's not her."

"It's Becky. She's trying to let you know she's all right. She's with you all the time."

"We have this floorboard at the top of the stairs in our house," I continue. "It creaks whenever anyone steps on it. That noise used to let me know that Becca had arrived home after a late night out. It became the source of a joke between us." I laugh in spite of myself. "Now, with Jake in Australia, it's only Bob and me in the house, but we keep hearing footsteps in the middle of the night, usually at one forty-five in the morning."

My next breath is deep and painful; the air burns as it presses into my lungs. "One forty-five—that was the time that Becca died."

"Becky's concerned about you. She says to tell you that she's all right. You don't have to worry about her. *I'm okay, Mom. I'm safe; I'm fine.*"

I hear the words as though they are coming from you, Rebecca.

"Becky didn't suffer," Karen assures me. "Her death came quickly. Becky didn't know what hit her."

Please let this be true. Please, God, I think.

"I get the sense that at first Rebecca was confused," Karen continues. "She wasn't expecting the accident, but she crossed over easily."

"I want to believe that. I can't stand the idea of Becky suffering."

"She didn't suffer. She's all right."

That's when I feel you, your presence wrapping around me like a soft, warm blanket.

"Becca says she wants you to take care of yourself. She wants you to go on with your life and not worry about her. *I'm all right, Mom. I'm all right.*"

"Are you really hearing her?" I ask.

Karen nods. "It's like vibrations that translate into words."

"There are times when I hear her, too," I offer. "Her voice is in my head telling me she's okay."

"Listen to that. It's real."

For the first time since we've begun talking, Karen looks away, past me, then off to the side, like she's seeing something just beyond my shoulder. She catches herself and focuses her attention back on me.

"What is it?"

She shakes her head, then looks beyond me again.

"What?" I press.

"She's right here with you. Rebecca is right here." Karen's voice is gentle, her eyes misty.

I turn to look, but all I see is the far end of the office and the window that opens to the outside.

When I thank Karen and marvel at how extraordinary it is to have this conversation, she tells me that we are being brought together for a purpose, that you are choreographing this. "Becky wants to reassure you," she says. "I never would have initiated this conversation on my own, but when you approached me, I decided it was okay."

Karen sighs. "There was a day not long after Becky's death. You came into the office, and Rebecca was with you. I thought about telling you that then, but wasn't sure how you would take it. She's been with you since her death. Becca loves you and wants you to take care of yourself."

"Then why do I hurt so much?"

"She's no longer a part of this world, not in the way she once was. You're her mother; you're mourning for your child. You need to allow yourself to grieve. I look at my two girls, and I can't imagine how you cope with Becca's death." Karen's eyes look so sad. "I don't know if you believe in angels, but I think Becky is an angel. She touched so many people's lives. I've never been at a funeral like hers. The emotion and energy Becca had was rare. So many people loved her."

I nod. "Recently, a friend of Jake's came over to the house to visit. We got to talking about Rebecca. I told him that for a long time I had believed that one of my children was going to die. At first, Aaron tried to explain it away as a natural fear. He pointed out that Becky was always one to test limits and that my typical reaction was to protect her by trying to control her. I insisted that he was wrong, that the sense of dread went way beyond my reaction to Becky testing me. I had been convinced that either Jake or Bec would die, and that thought terrified me."

"It would me as well," Karen agrees.

"A few months ago, Jake was offered a free trip to Israel. It was scheduled for winter break and was being sponsored by the Jewish youth movement. When he told me about the trip, I thought, *here it is; this is what I've been so afraid of.* Given the increase in terrorist activity in the Middle East, I worried about the risks. I begged Jake not to go, told him how worried I was, even argued that it was poor timing given his upcoming trip to Australia. I breathed easier when he finally decided against the Israel trip, telling myself that we had escaped the Fates."

Karen nods and waits for me to continue.

"My relief was short-lived. Becky was routinely staying out late at night with friends. When I voiced my concerns, she assured me that she was fine and insisted that nothing bad would happen. Two nights before she died, I couldn't sleep. After hours of lying awake, listening to Bob snore and watching him toss and turn, I went downstairs to the living room. I bundled up in a comforter and stretched out on the couch. I stayed awake for a long time, eventually going to the front window to see if Becky's car was out front." I shake my head at the memory. "It wasn't there. I found myself praying for her safety, but my fears got the best of me. I pictured a terrible accident with Becky dead on the side of the road. It wasn't until early morning that I finally dozed off. I awoke to find Bec upstairs, safe in her bed."

Karen and I both sigh. "Later that day, I talked with Becky about my worries when she would be out late. She tried to reassure me, promised that she's always careful. Then she apologized for frightening me, but said that she couldn't stay home with Bob and me every night. I had to accept her decision. She was far beyond the age of me being able to tell her what to do."

"There was nothing more you could have done."

"But we both knew. Becca and I both knew she was going to die."

Confused, Karen asks me to explain. I repeat the last conversation between us. You were going out with friends. I wanted to know when you'd be home, but you weren't sure. You didn't even know if you'd return that night or stay with a friend. Worried about your safety, I confided fears of you getting hurt or worse. You promised you would be okay and insisted that you didn't want to die. That might well have been the end of it, but I couldn't let it go. I expressed a concern about leaving the light on all night if you weren't coming home. How insane, to fret about wasting electricity! And then came your barbed response that keeps replaying in my head—you said that you hoped nothing would happen to you as you made your way from the car to the house.

"You can't undo any of this," says Karen. "Becky's all right now. She wants you to let it go. She loves you."

I want to believe that, and yet I can't shake the feeling that I'm responsible, that I let you die. I should have paid more attention, should have listened to my gut. I should have done something, anything to protect you. Why didn't I push harder, argue with you, demand that you stay home? I could have survived another argument, could have survived you being angry and frustrated with me. But this, you dying, I can't survive this!

The conversation with Karen shifts to your love of dragonflies, fairies, and butterflies. I tell her about dragonflies representing a connection to spirituality and a Higher Power. Karen suggests that they are a symbol of enlightenment. We talk about butterflies being linked to transformation and how the butterfly emerging from the cocoon is a symbol for breaking free. I wonder if that's what death has become for you, a way of becoming free.

I mention your father's visit to a psychic and share my concern about you now being with your birth mother.

"I don't think that Becky's birth mother has died," Karen says, "but either way, there's nothing for you to worry about. Becca knows who her mother is. She loves you."

I hope she is right about that.

"I wish that when Becky was alive that she knew how many people loved her," Karen continues. "Perhaps then she might still be alive. Perhaps that would have been enough to stop her from getting involved with friends who were so careless with her life."

Her thoughts mirror my own, but it is too late for wishes and what-ifs. None of those can bring you back to me. Nothing can.

*   *   *   *   *

Hero

The summer before third grade my mom became a hero. It all started when my family went camping at Lake Cachuma and we hiked up to a swimming hole called Red Rock. There were many families there. Some were sitting on rocks by the swimming hole, eating picnic lunches, and laughing. Some were diving off rocks or swinging off a rope into the deep blue water.

Unless you were in the very deepest part of the water there were rocks and boulders covering the bottom of the swimming hole. It took about one hour to drive to Red Rock after we got to the lake and then about twenty minutes to hike from the car to the swimming hole. We had planned to spend the whole day there with our friends and then return to the campground with them that evening.

We had spent two hours at Red Rock, enjoying ourselves. We swam in the refreshing water, had water fights, and sun bathed on rocks in the hot summer heat. Nobody seemed to be paying much attention to what was going on around them.

All of a sudden, out of the corner of my mom's eye, she saw a little boy's head going under the water. She quickly glanced around to see if anyone was going in after him. Nobody even seemed to notice that the little boy was in danger. My mom was up in a flash and running over uneven rocky terrain. She dove into the cool deep water. Within seconds she was carrying the boy up to the safety of the warm sandy beach.

The boy's mother grabbed her sobbing child from my mom and started screaming at her child, "Are you OK, are you OK?" The mother walked off to tend to her child without even saying thank you to my mom.

153

Meanwhile, my mom was hobbling up towards where my dad, my brother, and I were. I yelled, "Way to go, Mom!"

We all realized that the injury to her foot was much more serious than it seemed at first. Because of the serious sprain she wasn't able to walk for weeks. We were all proud because she saved someone's life. That's how my mom became a hero.

Rebecca, March 3, 1996

Twenty Seven

When it comes to death we human beings all live in an unwalled city.
Epicurus

I want others to rail against your death...

Two more days and you will have been gone for four months. One hundred and twenty days of missing you, of wishing things were different. One hundred and twenty days of remembering and thinking about what could have been.

I read through depositions from the survivors of the crash and learn that you didn't have much, if anything, to drink that night. I also discover that you often chose not to drink at all, even though your friends were making other decisions. That is something to be grateful for.

The D.A. calls with information about Tommie's blood alcohol level. He confirms that Tommie was intoxicated the night of the crash. That's it, then; Tommie will be found guilty of manslaughter. But the district attorney says it is not that simple. There are questions surrounding the blood draw. They still don't know what type of swab was used to clean Tommie's skin, whether it was an ethanol swab or isopropyl. If ethanol was used, that could have precipitated an elevation in the blood alcohol level, thereby making that figure questionable. There are also discrepancies between two existing sets of lab results.

The D.A. explains that one blood draw was done at the site of the crash and the other thirty to sixty minutes later at the hospital. In the intervening time, Tommie was given intravenous saline. Apparently, blood alcohol levels rise and descend rather than remaining stable, peaking sometime after ingestion. I take notes so that I can relay the information to the rest of the family. The D.A. promises that he will do his best to have Tommie convicted, but also cautions me about the possibility of Tommie going free.

Frustrated and angry, I hang up the phone. Doesn't anybody care that three people died at Tommie's hands?

*   *   *   *   *

Another week comes and goes without any more information. I throw myself into my work with the hope that it will distract me. My days are filled with performing psychological evaluations on teens who have been charged with crimes. The Court looks to me for recommendations. Ironic, isn't it? If Tommie were a few years younger and hadn't killed my daughter, his might be one of the cases crossing my desk.

Late in the day, I take a break to call the D.A. I tell myself that I'm searching for answers, but I already know the truth. The crash could easily have been avoided. If only Tommie had been sober. The real reason for my call is that I want justice. I can taste it, smell it. I delude myself into believing that it will bring me consolation. I want others to rail against your death. I want them to validate the despair and devastation that I live with every single day.

I dial the now familiar number. The D.A.'s voice is placid

as he informs me that they still have not decided whether or not to press charges. God, what is it going to take? I've been doing my homework, researching more information about alcohol and blood levels. I am prepared to do battle in order to get the information I want, but the attorney volunteers the exact numbers before I have a chance to press him.

I grab at a piece of scrap paper and scribble down notes as he explains that the swabs were isopropyl, thereby negating the possibility of a misleading elevation in the blood alcohol level. But there is still no word from the medical expert as to whether the intravenous saline given to Tommie on the way to the hospital could account for the drop in blood alcohol levels with the second sample. The first blood alcohol was .11, well over the legal limit of .08. The second blood alcohol was .04. Therein lies the problem. The obvious question is what, in fact, was Tommie's blood alcohol at the time of the crash? The district attorney suggests that I call him again in another two weeks. That seems like an eternity.

What I know in my heart is that Tommie was intoxicated at the time of the crash, but I wonder if the Court will see it that way? And beyond that, I can't help but question what you would want to see as the outcome of all this. Would you beg me to forgive Tommie or would you want him to be held accountable for what he has done?

I call friends and family and try to make sense out of the technical information I have been given. Some suggest that I consider a civil lawsuit. If the County ends up dropping the case, at least a civil suit would provide me with another way to go after Tommie.

Online, I research the dissipation rate of blood alcohol and attempt the calculations myself, working backward from the lowest blood count figure. This, and the legal machinations, serve as temporary distractions. They do nothing to change the reality of your death. My pain continues. There is no respite. God, look at how much Tommie has stolen from me!

Word travels fast in this town. I recently heard that Tommie is back home and has his driver's license. He's telling people there won't be any charges pressed against him. I call the D.A. who assures me that no decision has yet been made. He apologizes for the delay and explains that the people at the Crime Lab are continuing to work on Tommie's blood alcohol. I ask about Tommie's driver's license and after checking, the D.A. confirms that the license is active and in Tommie's possession. The attorney explains that he has no jurisdiction over the license; it falls to the Department of Motor Vehicles.

When I call the DMV, I am told that they are not at liberty to release any information.

"My daughter died in the crash," I tell the woman on the other end.

She falls silent, then says, "I'm sorry for that, but I still can't tell you anything."

"This man has already killed three people," I argue.

When she apologizes again, I demand to talk with a supervisor. Her tone is flat and controlled as she asks me for the date of the accident.

"Thanksgiving," I tell her. "The driver was Tommie Mercer." Then with more than a touch of anger, I say, "Do you need me to spell his name?"

"I know how to spell it," she says. "My friend's son was killed in that accident as well. The driver has his license?"

"Yes." My anger gives way to sadness. "That's what I'm told."

"Just a minute." She puts me on hold.

When she comes back on, she explains that she still can't give out any information, but promises that a supervisor will look into the matter.

It's a small victory, but for today it is enough. I have managed to do something constructive with my anger and grief.

*   *   *   *   *

My Greatest Desire

My greatest desire is to become a prima ballerina and an actress. I know it is going to take a lot of hard work and time to achieve these goals. I also know if I really work at it I can make it happen. Right now I am taking ballet classes on Monday, Wednesday, Friday, and Saturday. The classes last between one to three hours on these days. For acting I would like to take singing and acting classes when I have a little more time. This might be in the summer or when I am in college.

I think it would be fun to do dance or acting for a job because I am really interested in these things. I like playing different characters. I also like being the center of attention. I think it would be very stressful but I am positive that if I really keep at it I can achieve anything I want to.

Sometimes I do not really want to go to dance but my parents push me a little because they know that sometimes I do not always do the thing that is best for me to reach my goals. When I get there I have a blast. If it were not for them I do not think I could have come as far as I have already.

I know this is pretty weird but I can picture myself on a stage practicing for a center role in a performance. My hair would be in a low bun and I would be in tights and a leotard or an old T-shirt (one that has been used for lots of dancing) and sweats with the sweatshirt tied around my waist. I would have my pointe shoes on because I would be doing sotenu turns across the stage. I can see the director and the choreographer telling me to do the scene over again even though I did my best and put as much effort as I could into it. I would feel good because they are really watching and trying to make the performance the best it can be. I would also be tired and annoyed because I was trying so hard already. After many practices and hard

work the performance would be wonderful and a big success. I know I can achieve this goal. I am going to try super hard to make it happen.
    Rebecca, 1994

Twenty Eight

I turn my eyes to the mountains;
From where will my help come?
*   Psalm 121:1*

We connect, two mothers on opposite sides of the world...

The changing of the seasons from winter to spring takes me by surprise. Time has edged by so slowly that I was convinced that the world would forever be blanketed by cold, gray skies. With the warming days, I now question how it is that time has moved forward without you here. I have no desire to participate in this season of rejuvenation and awakening. That stands in such painful and awkward contrast to my grief. Springtime has become a cruel mockery.

Passover arrives. All of your cousins are home for the holiday. *Pesach* has always been one of my favorite times, but now, I wonder whether it will feel like cause for celebration. The rituals, the special foods, the prayers and stories that anchor the week do not hold the appeal that they once did.

Pesach marks another in a series of firsts without you. It marks the passage of more time since your death. I want the holiday over and done with. I want to hide from the unrelenting reminder that life goes on without you.

The evening before Passover, Bob and I call your brother in Australia to wish him a happy *Pesach*. Knowing that he is having a small *Seder* with newfound friends makes the distance between us easier to cope with. Though I would much prefer him to be home, at least I know that he won't be alone for the holiday.

For the last few years, Bob and I have hosted the *Seder*. Our home has been filled with all the commotion that goes along with the traditional dinner. But this year, the family has arranged to have the *Seder* at Grandma and Grandpa's. It doesn't matter where we observe Passover, my thoughts will turn to you. I will remember the way you would giggle with your cousins as all of you went through your comedic antics. I will remember how I used to admonish you and your young cohorts to pay attention to the rituals.

I plod through the beginning of the *Seder* with only marginal involvement, distancing myself in order to survive. I am grateful when Tahli takes charge of the service. It is easier, safer, to be an observer. It doesn't matter that she shortens the proceedings, picking and choosing what rituals to observe. I recite the prayers without conviction. *Strange*, I think, *how unconnected I am*. I don't even protest when the family opts out of singing many of the traditional songs.

Once the dishes are cleared and rinsed, I excuse myself, and make a quick exit for home. I don't want to linger and make conversation. I don't want to pretend that everything is normal or that I'm all right, because none of that is true.

The story of Passover speaks to the Jews coming out of slavery from Egypt. The Hebrew word for Egypt, *Mitzrayim*, is often taken to mean much more than the geographical location of the country. *Mitzrayim* is translated as a tight, narrow place and can be seen as being bound up or restricted either by our enemies or by our own distress. This Passover, I see no way out from the tight, narrow place in which I find myself. I am trapped, drowning.

At home, Bob and I watch television before going to bed. It is well before dawn when I awaken in tears with the realization that I am childless this Passover. You have died and Jake is in Australia. I feel lonely and abandoned. I rouse Bob and ask him to hold me, eventually falling back to sleep. I escape the memories that haunt me, if only for a short time.

*   *   *   *   *

Grandma loans me a book that one of her friends has suggested I read. *The Blessing of a Broken Heart* chronicles the journey of an Israeli woman, Sherri Mandell, in surviving the murder of her thirteen-year-old son. Mandell's agony is all too familiar. She has lived through the same hell in which I find myself.

As an Orthodox Jew, Sherri Mandell's practice of Judaism is far more traditional and conservative than mine. I don't care that she seems to follow the Torah in very literal ways, living by age-old traditions, many of which I have chosen to ignore. I don't care that our children died in different ways, at different ages. Like me, she is a mother who is grieving for her child. There is compassion and wisdom to be found in her writing. Her words become a lifeline for me, something to grab hold of to lift me out of the depths of these dark, swelling waters.

Mandell describes life in a small and insulated community in the West Bank of Israel. In her world, there are definite rules that determine the way one mourns. Her community forms a cocoon around her, buoying her up in those first days after her son's death.

Living in Southern California, I am surrounded by friends of varying backgrounds and faiths, friends with different rituals and ways to cope. There is no prescribed norm to tell me how to survive your death. Instead, I must choose the traditions I will adhere to.

As I come to the end of her book, I am left with the image of two distraught mothers who are consumed by grief. There is some relief in realizing that another woman has managed to survive a nightmare similar to my own. I understand, too, that Mandell has not followed a single, prescribed path as I would have anticipated. Instead, she has carved out an inspiring way to go on living in spite of her son's death. Rather than pushing the pain aside, she has managed to honor her grief by creating a retreat in her son's name, the purpose of which is to help others who are bereaved. She writes:

Being out of my home can feel like a trial. When I am out in Jerusalem one month after Koby's death with Daniel, trying to buy him shoes, I start to cry and stare into the shop window. He looks at me impatiently and sadly. Suddenly, I have an idea of how to cry without hurting or scaring him. I give him my watch: "Time me, give me one minute to cry." He times me, I cry for twenty-two seconds. After that day when I cry, I give my children my watch. It becomes a sort of game. "Give me one minute," I tell them. I usually cry for barely twenty seconds. They see that pain is something that you can enter and not be destroyed by. It's okay to cry, to be sad. Accepting my pain means that I don't have to be afraid of it. Neither do my children or husband. The pain sometimes feels like panic and fear, like madness. But if you can find a way to let it live, you can bear it without being broken. Then you can begin to heal, sewing your life back together one stitch at a time.

Sherri Mandell

It seems fitting that I read this book during the week of Passover. *The Blessing of a Broken Heart* offers me hope that I might free myself by embracing my grief rather than fighting against it. Perhaps this is to be my struggle, to accept your death and the emotional turmoil that comes with it and to figure out how to survive in spite of the pain. This may become my own version of leave-taking from *Mitzrayim*, setting out from the tight, constricted place. I consider that perhaps Passover still has a place in my life. It seems to me that *Pesach* has finally been redeemed and recaptured.

Rabbi Elisheva Beyer of Temple Beth Or in Reno, Nevada, writes:

> As a Jew, part of our work is to evolve our self: to keep growing and learning, especially Torah. The Sages tell us how important this work is that we do here in this world, noting that this world is like an entrance hall before the World to Come. They say, "Prepare yourself in the lobby (this world), that you may enter into the Palace (the World to Come)." Pirke Avot 4:21. Ultimately, leaving Mitzrayim means doing the work in this lifetime which is a prerequisite to entering the Palace.
>
> Rabbi Elisheva Beyer

To accept the pain that comes with you dying and then to move forward—these become my tasks, lessons I am to learn in this lifetime before following you to the Other Side. I take strength and encouragement from Rabbi Beyer's words, from Sherri Mandell's words.

Days after finishing *The Blessing of a Broken Heart*, I write to Sherri Mandell. I tell her about your death and thank her for sharing her own story. I let her know that her book has brought me comfort and offered me some hope of again being able to enjoy life. She writes back, expressing her sadness for my loss and thanking me for my words. We connect, two mothers on opposite sides of the world, but with a common bond. Life brings comfort in unanticipated ways, sometimes from an Orthodox woman who is 7500 miles away.

*   *   *   *   *

Reanne Singer

Star of David
Glistening and bright
Committed to Judaism
Values and morals
A way of life
Belief in a higher spirit
Finding out who I am.

Rebecca, December 6, 1996

Twenty Nine

Our life is a faint tracing on the surface of mystery.
Annie Dillard, Pilgrim at Tinker Creek

There will be pink roses...

Many years ago, I was given a set of Tarot cards. I wrapped the cards in a silk scarf and stored them in a small wood box that sat on a table in the living room. The cards remained untouched until a few months before your death. Wanting to understand more about the cards, I read a few books and tried my hand at Tarot. But interpreting the cards was far more complicated than I had anticipated.

A month or so later, you asked that I read Tarot for you. We sprawled out on the living room floor with the box of cards between us. Your face was filled with anticipation as I unwrapped the cards from the eggplant-colored scarf. The reading touched on your relationship with a man. It suggested that he was out for himself rather than having your best interests at heart. I skirted around this, believing that the reference was to your boyfriend, David.

After you and David ended the relationship, I confessed

what I had seen in the cards. Now, I wonder if I misunderstood the throw. Were the cards saying something about Tommie instead? Was there a warning for us in that reading?

A week or so later, you again asked me for a reading. The spread frightened me. The death card sat in the position of your future. I searched for a palatable interpretation, something less ominous than what I sensed. I did my best to hide my concern. I combed through my books and grabbed hold of more abstract interpretations. I talked with you about the symbolism of doors closing and others opening, of new opportunities and chances for growth appearing after difficult changes. You seemed satisfied. I wanted to be as well but was filled with dread.

I put the cards away and did not return to them for many months. As much as I tried to dismiss the reading, it continued to haunt me.

Now, with your passing, my thoughts return to that throw of the cards. Was there something I could have done to prevent your death? Should I have told you what I saw in the cards that day? Perhaps that would have protected you. Perhaps you would still be alive today.

*   *   *   *   *

Months after your death, a colleague's husband offers to read Tarot for me. Within days, I am at Lisa and Ron's house with Ron seated across from me at their kitchen table. Having spent years learning Tarot, Ron is far more sophisticated and astute than I am. I try to be patient as I watch him study the throw. I focus on his hands—large and dark brown, splayed flat against the yellow linoleum table.

When he looks up, his face and eyes are sad and resigned. "This center card, here," he says, pointing at a heart that is pierced by swords. "It's obvious, isn't it? Your heart has been broken by Becky's death. But the cards tell me more than that. I think you're going to have some future success with your writing."

Before your death, this comment would have made me giddy with anticipation. But right now, Ron's assurance is uninspiring.

"You're going to be involved in some legal action," he continues. "I'm not sure what that's about, just legal action." He examines the cards again. "You will find peace and happiness."

Yeah, right, I want to say. *In which lifetime?* But I avoid the sarcasm.

As he continues on, I become more aware of your presence. "Becky wants you to know that she's okay. Rebecca is fine. She's safe." Ron no longer looks at the cards, but at me.

By this point, Lisa has walked in. I glance over at her and then back at Ron.

"Becky's sad because you're sad," he says. "But she's all right. She passed through quickly and easily. She went straight through. It was her time. Both of you knew this was coming. You and Rebecca knew she was going to die."

Where is this coming from? I've never talked with him about these things.

His speech is more pressured. "Rebecca has lived many lifetimes. She doesn't want you to worry about her, wants you to go on with your life, says the two of you will be together soon enough."

Lisa hasn't moved from the corner of the room.

"There's an older woman with her," Ron adds. "Someone who welcomed Becky after her passing." He struggles for the woman's name. He repeats the "*m*" sound with different vowel pronunciations; "*Ma, Mi, May,* is it *May, Ma*? I don't know. She's there helping Rebecca."

I lean forward. The muscles in my hands and arms are tight. *I have to do this right,* I think. *I have to understand so that Ron will keep talking, so that Becky will keep talking. I can't disrupt*

169

this energy.

"My grandmother, Min," I offer. "We used to call her Mom. Is that who you're referring to? Or maybe my mother's friend, Magda?"

Ron shrugs. "I don't know. *Ma, May?* I can't quite get it. There's an older man, too, a real character—bald head, cigar, drove a Cadillac, maybe. He and the woman are teasing Becky, laughing with her, helping her. And there's another woman sitting in a rocking chair—lots of jewelry, she likes jewelry. She's much more prim and proper than the first woman. The man keeps giving this second woman a hard time, tells her: *Lighten up, you old broad.* He looks like a Buddha, maybe that's because of the bald head."

I run through who these people might be. *Is it Max?* I wonder to myself, considering a good friend of Grandma and Grandpa's who died a number of years ago. Max was loud and abrupt with a dry sense of humor. It would be like him to talk the way Ron is describing. Besides, Max was bald and used to remind me of a Buddha. My thoughts go to the second woman Ron referred to, the one with the jewelry. That sounds like my maternal grandmother, Sylvie.

I sneak a look at Lisa who is staring at her husband.

"A great-uncle?" Ron suggests. He shrugs again as though questioning his own conclusion.

Is he still talking about the same man or are we now on to someone else? I consider my Grandma Min's younger brother. Uncle Joe was this short pistol of a guy with a shock of white hair that framed not only his face, but also the bald spot on the crown of his head. He smoked a cigar and used to make it look like the smoke was coming right out of his ears. Uncle Joe could even blow the smoke into circles that floated upward in lazy rings. I can imagine him trying to ease the tension, telling my grandmother to *lighten up.* Is it possible that Ron is honing in on two souls and perceiving them as one? Maybe he's seeing both Uncle Joe and Max.

Now, Ron is off on a tangent. "There's a little dog there with her, a little black dog, like Toto or something. No," he says, changing his mind, "a little black terrier, funny looking, ugly, little black dog."

Crying now, I wonder how he knows about Phoenix. I've never told him about your childhood pet.

"Who's he talking about?" Lisa asks me.

"It's Becky's dog," I explain. "We had Phoenix from the time Becca was little." I wipe at my eyes and nose. "When Becca was seventeen, Bob and Jake and I went to Mammoth for a few days. Wanting to be with her friends, Bec chose to stay behind. Phoenix was really old. While we were away, Phoenix became terribly sick. Bec took her to the vet and had to deal with her being put down."

Ron seems not to hear the exchange between Lisa and me. "Rebecca wants you to write your book," he says. "*Make it to the bestseller list, Mom. I'll be there with you. I'll help you. Write your book.*"

"I've never seen him like this," Lisa observes.

As if not having heard her, Ron says, "*It's important. It's going to touch many people. I'll be there with you.*" He pauses for a breath. There is no question for me that he is communicating your words rather than his own, Rebecca.

But when he continues, it again seems to be his voice, not yours. "There's something about pink roses," he says. "You're going to get a big bunch of pink roses. Those are often a sign from the Other Side. The roses will be Rebecca's signal to you that she's all right. You'll know from the roses that she's okay. There will be pink roses, many roses." He gestures with a broad sweep of one arm.

"I don't know if they're real or ceramic or something," he adds, again referring to the flowers. "You'll know when you get them. You have to let me know. You call me when you get the roses."

"Maybe it's pink azaleas," I suggest, flashing on a plant

my father had given me days earlier.

"No!" Ron flares. "It's not azaleas. It's roses. She says it's roses! You'll know it when you see them."

My thoughts race. Last night, Bob had considered bringing me flowers. But he had abandoned the idea after I called him at the office to remind him that we were going to call Jake in Australia. Had Bob planned on bringing me pink roses?

"Things don't usually happen this way," Ron continues. "Right now, there's this rush of vibrations, kind of at the back of my neck. There's this *whoosh*, and then I'm hearing and seeing things."

Still at her post by the sink, Lisa watches us.

"Are you really seeing Rebecca?" I ask Ron.

"It's not that simple." Again he explains about the rush of vibrations preceding him being able to see and hear you. Then he qualifies that, stating that it's not the same as when we see or hear one another. "They're making their presence known from the Other Side," he says. "They have to do it in a way that we can perceive."

He is quiet. Is he waiting for my reaction? But when I don't respond, he says, "It's not like they're still in the same form as they were when they were alive, but they're trying to give us access through our perceptual world. So, yes, I'm seeing images, but they're vague compared to the way you or I normally see things."

He looks away and shifts his weight in the chair. "I can't get her name. The other woman, I can't get her name. There's *Ma* or *May* and the other woman who's so serious. The man tells her to lighten up. And the woman, I don't know..." He repeats himself. His speech is pressured. Is he now referring to a third woman?

With gaze riveted on me, he leans forward. I'm unnerved by his intensity. "Rebecca says: *Go ahead with the lawsuit, Mom. I won't be angry with you. Go ahead with the suit. It's my gift to you.*"

"Okay," I sputter. I haven't mentioned the possibility of a lawsuit to either Lisa or Ron.

"There will be pink roses," he says again. "You need to pay attention to the pink roses. You'll know when you get them. Rebecca will bring you pink roses. At the foot of a bed or next to a bed."

I want to ask him what bed? Where am I supposed to look? Is bed even the word Ron said? Did I hear it wrong? Did he misunderstand?

"Pink flowers," he repeats. "You'll know when they arrive. Rebecca says they will be a sign from her." He draws in a breath before changing direction. "She loves Bob. The arguments were only teenage angst and not liking someone new being in the picture. She really does love him, though. And there's something about a term paper. Becky says to look for the seventh or eighth grade paper. That will help you with your writing. I'm seeing an old manila folder or envelope, a yellowed folder or envelope. It's there. The paper is there."

"Hers or mine?" I ask.

"Hers. Becky wants you to look for her paper. It will help you with your writing. *You need to get the word out,* she says. *Write the book. Write the book, Mom. I'll help you.*"

What paper is he talking about? I remember you writing a report about dolphins and another about the California mission, but I can't imagine that either of those is the one I'm supposed to look for.

"*You can tell Dad this stuff if you want, but he won't get it. Dad doesn't get it. He isn't open to this. I keep giving him signs, but he doesn't see them. He doesn't understand. Dad's okay, but he doesn't get all this.*"

Then, in apology, Ron adds, "I don't even know your ex-husband. I'm sorry if I hurt your feelings by saying this, but I'm getting the strong image of someone who is clinical or analytical. He isn't open to Rebecca's signs. He's like this..." Ron crosses his arms in front of his chest and scrunches his eyes shut.

Then his eyes pop open. "The pink roses," he insists. "When the pink roses arrive, you'll know that they are from Rebecca. I think that's it." He hoists himself from the chair and quickly walks out of the room.

"Do you know what he means by the roses or the paper?" Lisa asks.

"No," I tell her.

We go out to the living room, but Ron isn't there.

"He probably went outside for a smoke," Lisa explains.

As I gather up purse and keys and prepare to leave, Lisa invites me to stay for dinner. She's determined for me to call Bob at the office and have him join us. Feeling the need for some time to myself, I suggest that I'll go home for a while and return later.

As I head for the door, Ron returns. "It's Phyllis," he announces. "Does that name mean anything to you?"

Dizzy and lightheaded, I brace myself against a nearby wall. Lisa is at my side, wrapping an arm around me. "Phyllis was my mother's best friend," I explain. "She died a few years ago from lung cancer."

"It was Phyllis," Ron repeats. "She's there with Rebecca. She says: *My name is Phyllis.*"

As my tears return, I wonder if they are a reflection of sadness or relief in hearing that Becky is with someone I adored and trusted.

Once home, I need to surround myself with as much of you as I can. I hurry to your room. I breathe in the details of what is left of you—photos of family and friends, figurines of dragonflies and fairies, artwork on the walls.

"I love you," I say. "I miss you, Rebecca."

I run a hand over your bedspread and pillows. My gaze wanders across your cabinet shelves and settles on two jewelry boxes. I move the smaller one aside and stare at a larger rectangular box that is covered in light pink corduroy fabric with a spray of roses in varying shades of cream, pink, and crimson.

"My God, is this it?" I whisper. "Pink roses. There are pink roses here!"

I have looked through this box so many times since your death, but now, as I again open the lid, I discover a plastic floor at the bottom. I lift out the shelf to unearth a hidden layer of treasures. I retrieve a small porcelain figurine and deposit it in the palm of my other hand. The figure is a ballet dancer that is missing one arm. I study the clean break. The symbolism of the broken body is not lost on me. I flash on images of you and the crash, picture the way your body must have looked when you died—twisted, broken, bruised.

Of course, by this point I am crying again. With vision blurred, I pour through the contents of the box. That's when I spot another dancer dangling from a thin chain. She is posed in a *gran jeté*, your favorite ballet move. Years ago, I tried to execute a *gran jeté* like yours. The jump didn't go well. I was clumsy and awkward, but my attempt made us both laugh.

I unearth more treasures—a pendant of a little girl, a number of six-pointed Stars of David given to you when you became a *Bat Mitzvah*, and a necklace with a charm that says *I love you* in sign language.

This day is full of blessings.

*   *   *   *   *

If I could have a secret power I would have invisibility. I picked invisibility because I think it would be cool to watch people and other stuff without them knowing I'm there.

But the thing is that I wouldn't want to be like this forever because I couldn't see my family or friends. Well, I could see them but they couldn't see me and I never want to lose either of them. They're both very special.

Rebecca, November 22, 1993

Thirty

If you live in this world and are not merely passing through it, you will have to listen to what stirs your soul. The journey itself—exhausting, exhilarating, and wondrous—will begin to enchant you, and courage will carry you past the objections of those who will not understand.

Rabbi David Wolpe, Why Be Jewish?

Finding pieces of you that have been here all along...

The belief that you are safe is not an easy one to sustain. As the days pass, my conviction falters. Yet again, I worry about you. I wonder where you are, how you're doing, what you're thinking and feeling. Is this my fate, to endlessly fret about my child?

The weekend looms before me. It's your grandfather's birthday, and we are planning a small celebration. The numbers for the party have dwindled with many of your cousins away at school and others in the family out of town. I wonder if they have sought out other activities in an attempt to escape one more get-together without you.

This will be Grandpa's first birthday without you. The

firsts all seem to create an endless lineup of hurdles that seem to define the year. We have already made it through my birthday as well as yours. We've made it through New Years and Passover. How many more *firsts* must we confront?

When my back goes out, Bob is left to organize the birthday party on his own. He tends to the preparations and provides Grandpa with as much of a celebration as the family seems able to tolerate. The next day my back is no better. Bob is at the computer. Not wanting to be by myself, I stretch out on a nearby couch in the office. At my request, Bob pulls out a large cardboard box where I have stored your childhood artwork and writings. He slides it near me so that I can rummage through the contents. My hope is that I will find the seventh or eighth grade paper that Ron has suggested I look for.

At two feet tall, one foot wide, and maybe three or four feet long, the box overflows with art projects, essays, poems, and birthday cards. I sift through these reminders of you. Buried deep within the box is a loosely bound book. My heart races as I read the first page: *My Autobiography, Written and Illustrated by Rebecca Amy Singer-Beilin*. With trembling hands, I turn the page and read through the *Acknowledgements*:

> *I would like to thank my Mom, Reanne Singer, and my Dad, Bob Beilin, for their help and support in getting this project completed and in helping me to be the person I am today. I also thank my teacher, Mrs. Olson, for her advice on making this project a success. I would also thank my friend Ariana Rothstein-Fisch and my relatives for believing in me and helping me through this project.*

Bob looks over and asks if I have found what I was searching for.

"Yes," I tell him. I hold up your autobiography as though it's a trophy. I am careful not to let my tears splotch the brightly-colored pages.

After handing me a box of tissues and giving me a kiss,

he leaves, allowing me space and solitude as I immerse myself in your words. I read through the essay in which you talk about your name and how it came to be yours. What a tremendous gift you have given me in these writings, Becca. Then I am on to the next entry where you write about your greatest desires and how you envisioned your future. I find the family tree we assembled together and remember the many questions you had for your father and me and your grandparents. After scanning the list of the hundred things you thought would be necessary to have a successful life, I happen upon a picture of you at age seven or eight. You are beaming; your eyes look back at me as though nothing is wrong in our world. How easy it would be to let myself fall into the belief that everything is fine and as it should be, that you are alive and well, simply grown up and living on your own.

Bob returns to find me still in tears. He suggests that I put the memory box away for a while, maybe come back to it at a later time, but I am determined to grab hold of as many memories as I can.

I pore over your words, ingesting every syllable, every punctuation mark. I read your essay about my Grandma Min and then an assignment entitled *Evidence of My Life*.

Hours later, it is enough. I secure your writings and artwork back in the memory box. I had always assumed that we were holding on to these keepsakes for you. Now, I realize that I am the one to benefit from these treasures. I picture a time in the future, after Jake has his children. I will open this box and share these parts of you with them. I'll tell my grandchildren about the radiant, graceful girl who was their aunt. I will talk to them of your hopes and dreams. I promise that they will know who you were.

That night, I fall asleep with more ease than I have in many months. The next day, Bob reports that he was awake during much of the night, listening to your footsteps in the hall outside our room. Once again, we are reminded that you are determined to make your presence known. We know you are close by, sweet girl, comforting and reassuring us. How could we not?

Immersing myself in memories of you has been good. The memories have become a way to heal. Finding pieces of you that have been here all along brings me comfort. Setting boundaries around my grief, creating time and space for the sadness and then putting it aside for a bit, seems like a healthy step. Embracing my grief has made it less overwhelming. Perhaps Sherri Mandell was right. I again consider her words about pain feeling like madness:

...if you can find a way to let it live, you can bear it without being broken. Then you can begin to heal, sewing your life back together one stitch at a time.

Sherri Mandell

* * * * *

Rebecca

Happy, smart, nice, friendly
Relative of Uncle Bruce and Aunt Leslie
Lover of dancing, family, pets
Who learned from teachers, family, friends
Famous for dancing
Who used to dream of
Being a professional horseback rider
Who now dreams of being an actress and a singer
Who fears earthquakes, fires, and someone hurting me and my family
Who would never hurt my family, friends, or my dogs
Who needs family, love, and friends
Who feels safe and loved
Who wishes for peace in the world and no homework
Resident of Ventura, California
Singer-Beilin

Rebecca, 1993

Thirty One

A great sorrow, like a mariner's quadrant, brings the sun at noon down to the horizon, and we learn where we are on the sea of life.
Henry Wadsworth Longfellow, "Table-Talk", Driftwood

I find myself transformed by the sorrow...

My grief is quieter now, filled less with frenzy and desperation and more with subdued resignation. I awaken with these words in my head. They linger throughout the morning. After writing them down on a scrap of paper, I keep them close at hand over the next two weeks and read them often.

My grief is changing. In the days and weeks following your death, my despair seemed so intense that I imagined it being able to swallow me up, leaving behind only the skeletal remains of the person I once was. That has changed. Now, I find myself transformed by the sorrow. You, who were so enamored of butterflies, fairies, and dragonflies, have given me the gift of these symbols of transformation. Rather than allowing my grief to destroy me, I try to accept it and make it a part of who I am. I re-evaluate what is important in life and question the meaning of existence. It all sounds very mystical, but these changes hit at my very core. I look at myself and the world around me in different and challenging ways.

I used to fantasize about your future, wanting to envision where life would take you. Like most mothers, I was filled with so many hopes and dreams. That, too, has changed. Now, I am filled with questions: *Where are you? What comes after death, and how is that for you? Are you at peace?* I wonder if you miss me, if you miss the life you had here with us.

There are no answers, but with every passing day, I believe more strongly in your continued existence. It is a matter of faith, of what I know in my heart. Our time here is limited and precious. How often have I heard people say that we need to live every day to the fullest? Now, I am trying to do that. I remind myself to count my blessings, to savor the moments I have with the people I love.

When I visit with Grandma and Grandpa, I am struck by the cadence of age in their voices. *Enjoy the conversations,* I think. *Grandma and Grandpa won't be here forever.* There is so much that I have taken for granted.

I wander through the house and notice one picture after another that chronicles our family's life. In the hallway outside my bedroom are photos of you and your brother as young children. The picture of you as a newborn takes me back to those early days. And there is the photo of you as a toddler draped across your favorite stuffed animal, the furry monkey that was every bit as big as you were. Another picture—you at age two, perched atop a bright orange tractor. I smile through my tears. The photo that brings so much joy is the one of me pregnant with Jake, my shirt pulled up to expose my swollen belly, and you facing me, puffing out your tummy to mimic mine. I had my beautiful girl and another baby growing inside me.

More photos in the living room. I love the one of you and Jake on a tire swing at our old house. Both of you had a wonderful time flying through the air. In another, you are dressed up in a ballet outfit with pink tights, leotard, and matching tutu. You are making one of your dramatic entrances. My attention shifts to a picture of you and Tahli hugging. At ages thirteen and eight, you were filled with affection for each other.

I want more pictures, more memories. I had so looked forward to lining my shelves with photos of you as a bride and as a young mother, Rebecca. I wanted to share in every stage of your life. But you and I share something different now. We share your death, your leave-taking. Still, I wish for what we once had. I wish for everything that could have been.

You were so full of opinions and strong emotions. Your passionate words collided with my own bullheadedness. And yet, in the end, there was always reconciliation. Both of us offered up apologies and heartfelt *I love yous*.

It's quite amazing how different you and your brother were from one another. Jake's quiet introspection was the counterpoint to your exuberance and outspoken nature. That's not to say that you couldn't be contemplative as well, but you wanted to process and talk things through far more than he did. I used to joke with you and suggest that you pursue law as a career. Your tenacity and ability to dissect an issue would have served you well as a litigator.

I miss your words and the passion that was so much a part of who you were. I long for the mother-daughter talks that could stretch for hours, late into the night. Remember how we would stretch out on my bed, weary from school and work, and talk endlessly about the day's happenings? We would discuss school and relationships, family, career choices, whatever seemed important at the time. No matter the topic, I could always be sure you would demand honesty and a significant chunk of time. There was no quitting prematurely, no putting the issues aside for another time. You would not tolerate that. On occasion, Jake would join us, at least until he tired of the marathon. Then he'd retreat to television, the computer, or a book—something more peaceful than our prolonged talks.

I can't help but wonder if you're still sorting things through. That's what I'm doing. Since your death, I dig through the memories of our past. I unravel the details, search for patterns, then reshape these strands of our lives into shapes that offer some answers.

I look forward to the times when I'm the only one at home. I enjoy these solitary moments when I'm free of other distractions and demands. The quiet provides space for me to connect with you. If I listen carefully, I can hear you. Your voice, your laughter—I want to capture these sounds, hold them in the palm of my hand and close my fingers around them so that they can't disappear.

Keep allowing me to hear her voice, I pray. *Don't let this remnant of her vanish.* I find some comfort in the idea that your voice is inside of me.

*   *   *   *   *

My Coat of Arms

For my coat-of-arms I chose a heart, my family, a peace sign, a happy face, the ocean, and ballet shoes. I chose these things because they all have something to do with me.

I chose a heart because it represents love. Love is important to me because if I did not give or receive it other people would be unhappy and so would I. If there was not love the world would be a really lonely place and everyone would be feeling bad all the time. I included my family on the coat-of-arms because they are very important to me. A family also involves love.

I put a happy face on my coat-of-arms because it represents happiness. I think happiness is very important because if you do not have any happiness you would only feel anger or sadness. I have a lot of happiness in my life and I am very glad that I do. I would have a pretty boring life without happiness.

I also included the ocean on my coat-of-arms because I spend some of my time there. When I do, I have a blast. I love to body-surf, boogie board, make sand castles, and most of all, just play in the water. It is really fun to go on the rocks and look for sand crabs, star fish, and lots more. Sometimes a friend and I will go and take a run on the beach. We have gone all the way from the park to the pier. It is a great way to get energy out, exercise, and just be with a friend.

As you can see I drew ballet shoes also. I chose these because I spend a lot of my time dancing. Dance is very important to me because it is a great way for me to release anger and get exercise also. Dance is one of my favorite things to do.

For my coat-of-arms I put things on it that are important to me. I think they help to describe who I am. Now I know more about a coat-of-arms and why people used them in the olden days.

Rebecca, 1993

Becca at 1 with Monkey

Becky at 2 with Reanne

Becca at 13 with Tahli

Thirty Two

The secret of seeing is to sail on solar wind. Hone and spread your spirit, till you yourself are a sail, whetted, translucent, broadside to the merest puff.

Annie Dillard, Pilgrim at Tinker Creek

Your laughter slides through the air...

My grief returns. I slip into the protective cocoon of your sweatshirt and run from the house, more comfortable in the night's darkness. I settle on a rocker on the front porch. My throat fills with sobs; the primitive sound is rooted deep inside of me.

And then your voice is floating toward me through the darkness. *"It's all right,"* you tell me. *"I'm here, Mom. It's okay."*

Across the front lawn, I see you at age eighteen, your lean body stretched out on the grass as you soaked up the sun. Your tawny skin had deepened to mocha brown, putting you well ahead of the rest of us with a summer tan. Once again, you pull your dirt-splattered car on the lawn, just the way you did that day after you had gone hiking in the nearby mountains of Ojai. You convince me to help you wash the

Volvo. Once it's soaped and rinsed, you tell me that the windows should be rubbed down with newspaper to avoid any smudges or watermarks. What a fun time we had washing your car, spraying one another with the hose, and then drying off in the sun.

I look to another part of the yard and see you at age ten, your body lanky and graceful as you fly through the air in a series of *gran jetés*. How you glowed when you danced.

At fourteen, you managed to convince your father and me that you would do better with contact lenses than cumbersome glasses. Do you remember that day when one of the lenses fell out, seemingly swallowed up by the dense grass? You enlisted your brother and me to help you find the missing lens. On hands and knees we carefully combed the front lawn, but at the end of a long hour, I finally gave up. Jake continued to help you. You were thrilled when he found the missing lens.

The night is quiet. No one else is about.

Through the darkness, I hear you whisper, "*I love you.*"

"I love you, too," I answer.

Those were the last words we spoke to one another. The night of the crash, you were heading out to meet your friends. I stood at the front door and watched you walk to your car.

You turned and smiled, said, "*I love you.*"

Again I hear you whisper.

"I love you, too," I tell you, repeating the words over and over again, as though in prayer.

Having you close like this is a blessing; but even still, it isn't enough. I want more of you. I yearn for the sound of your incessant chatter. I crave the laughter and the arguments. I want to hear you calling to me from the far end of the house. I want to be inconvenienced by your demands for my attention. I want your energy, your passion for life. These short-lived visits don't take the place of having you alive and in this world with me.

Bob has wandered out to the porch with the dogs.

190

Noticing that I am upset, he asks if there's anything he can do.

"I miss her," I tell him. "I want to undo Rebecca's death."

"Yes," he agrees.

The dogs stay close, edgy as they press their muzzles against my legs.

"Re's just sad," Bob tells them. "She'll be okay."

Your voice blows in again. Your laughter slides through the air. I imagine it lifting, buoyed on warm currents. I catch sight of you as a young girl leading the flock of other children from the family up the street.

"I'm okay, Mom. I'm all right. I love you."

You are close now, right up against me. I feel you, sense you. I tilt my head toward you and close my eyes to the rest of the world.

"Don't go yet," I plead. "I need you here awhile longer."

"I'm here." The words wash over me.

Later that night, I find Rocky in your room, sniffing around as though he's searching for something. Ever since your death, he has avoided your room, at times even refusing to go in there at all. Now, I watch as he inspects the open closet and then walks around your bed with his nose to the ground.

Offering reassurances, I tell him what you have told me, that you're all right. Has he, too, sensed your presence this evening? We all miss you, Rebecca. We want you home.

*   *   *   *   *

A few nights ago, I found myself in the house alone. Bob was still at work, the dogs in the yard. Perched on one of the lower stairs, I had a clear view into the living room. I remembered how much you loved to dance out there, transforming the hearth into your very own stage. Your slender frame flew down the length of the room. With a look of jubilation, you propelled yourself into the air like a weightless fairy.

191

Your absence is almost unbearable. The pain of it forces me to look away. But as I do that, I spot a flicker of movement off to the side. I turn. Nothing. I look away again, but something shifts. You flit past.

"Show me," I whisper.

More movement. I know you are here with me. The light changes over by the hearth, and I see a blurred shape, its dimensions moving the way that fog does. It is as though I am looking at the world through a bit of ocean glass. I know what is on the other side of the glass, but the outline and form are altered, unfamiliar. I think about dust particles suspended in the air. When the light catches them just right, I'm allowed a momentary glimpse of the particles moving about. And I think about the Jewish notion of the veil that separates our world from the next, from the world to come or *Olam Haba*.

Dara Horn speaks to this in an interview about her novel, *The World to Come*:

"The world to come" is a phrase with multiple meanings. It's used in the Jewish tradition to mean a future redemptive age, which is often conflated with life after death. But there are also elements of Jewish legend that discuss a life before birth—and for those who haven't yet been born, I realized, the world we live in now is the world to come. And for all of us, the world to come is literally just the future.

...in the Talmud and one or two other sources, variations on the following legend appear: Before a person is born, he is taught the entire Torah. When he is informed that he is about to be born, he doesn't want to leave this paradise of knowledge. So an angel slaps him on the face, under the nose, causing him to forget everything he has learned (and causing the dent that we all have just below our noses). He is then born completely ignorant, and he is forced to spend the rest of his life trying to remember what he has forgotten.

Dara Horn interviewed by Elizabeth Glixman

I fully believe that you have allowed me a glimpse of you in the world to come, Rebecca. I decide not to tell many people about this experience. I don't want to have to deal with them dismissing it as an expression of my grief. I don't want them to suggest that I've imagined this out of desperation. I don't want to hear their disbelief, their challenges of my reality. I know that I have seen you. It is a matter of faith; it is my truth. Your presence soothes me, consoles me.

*   *   *   *   *

Do You Remember?

Do you remember me, think of me
in those quiet, solitary moments
or when your soul is filled
with ripples of laughter
washing in like waves upon the shore

Do you remember the ocean
the cold salt water upon your skin
the rush of wind against your face
you flying across the sand
running down that wide expanse of beach

Do you remember
a shimmering summer's day
the sky blue and cloudless
the sun warming your body
turning your skin to mocha brown

Do you still smell the rain
those first moments as it falls to earth
the anticipation
the joy
the world bathed anew

Do you remember my arms
wrapped around you, holding you close
the rhythm of my heartbeat
against your silk-soft, baby's cheek
you dozing, soothed and rocked toward dreams

Do you know that I carry your essence
in my heart
images from our past
now fill my waking hours
haunt my dreams

Remember me often, my darling
with smiles and laughter
tears and love
remember me often
I remember you
      All my love, Mom, February 25, 2007

         *   *   *   *   *

    I'm so excited. Yesterday I got my pointe shoes for dance. I think they are really pretty; they are a peachy-pink color. They have a silk ribbon. I have been dancing for 11 years and I finally got on pointe! I think it is so cool. Now I can dance on the tip of my toes. I also got a dance skirt which is a silk skirt that you can only use when you are dancing. Mine is black. I also got some pads to stick in the tips of the shoes so when I get up on them it won't hurt my toes.
    Rebecca, October 18, 1993

Thirty Three

Accepting the pain of living, knowing one's heart will—and should—be broken, is the beginning of wisdom.
  Rabbi David Wolpe, Making Loss Matter

Anger seemed to be your way to separate. What was mine?

The dependency of your childhood gave way to an adolescence that descended with undeniable force. You were determined to define yourself as separate from me. Convinced that I was overprotective and at times paranoid about keeping you and your brother out of harm's way, you pursued a campaign for more and more freedom. Of course, I knew that from a developmental perspective you were doing exactly what you were supposed to, but it was difficult for me as a parent to balance out your need for freedom against my need to keep you safe.

Remember when you convinced me to let you go downtown with friends? We agreed that you would stay on Main Street to explore the thrift stores and artsy shops rather than venturing down the less-traveled side streets that led to the beach. In retrospect, I shouldn't have been surprised that you and your friends ended up on the boardwalk. The three of you wandered into the newly built parking structure to check out the view of the coastline from three stories up. The tall parking structure was something new and exciting for our quiet town.

There are times when life dishes out just consequences. You and Daena and Kathy rode the elevator to the top of the building and drank in the view, but on the ride down, the elevator jammed. Stuck in the tiny space for thirty minutes, the three of you began to panic, filling the time with melodramatic tears coupled with hugs and heartfelt goodbyes just in case the elevator plummeted to the ground and you didn't survive. It must have seemed an anticlimactic ending when you were freed by a maintenance man.

I was less than sympathetic to what you had endured. Rather than sympathizing with your plight, I objected to you breaking our agreement. The consequence was that you lost the privilege of going out with your friends for a few weeks.

By fifteen, you were going downtown more often. You told me about meeting an eighteen year old guy. You said the two of you were friends; that was all. I worried that one or both of you had other things in mind. I was uncomfortable with the age difference and the issue that I knew nothing about Chris, other than the fact that you had met him downtown and that he supposedly worked for a small business that dealt in baseball cards. I tried to stop you from talking with him, but you balked at my rules, sneaking phone calls and secret meetings.

The Chris situation escalated the evening you announced that he was taking you out to eat. Tempers flared when I told you not to leave the house. I stood at the front door and blocked your exit. You held your ground and insisted that I move out of the way. I didn't physically stop you but told you that if you left with him, I would call the police. I also suggested that you tell Chris that if he laid a hand on you, he would be charged with statutory rape or molestation.

I watched from the front window as you stomped out to his waiting car. A few minutes later, you traipsed back into the house and slammed the door behind you. Chris drove off in a huff. That was the last we ever saw of him. You were beyond angry, but you were safe. That was all that mattered.

*   *   *   *   *

The months before your death were tumultuous for you and me. One minute we were getting along and the next we were embroiled in yet another conflict. The last night we had together was no different. At twenty-two, you continued to struggle to establish your autonomy. You resisted my attempts to control you. The closeness, and perhaps the dependency we had on one another, was both a blessing and a curse. Anger seemed to be your way to separate. What was mine? Looking back, I wish we had handled our challenges more gracefully.

Not too long ago, we went to Aunt Allie's for dinner. Jake had arrived there before us, having spent the afternoon with Bria. Since Allie's house was only a few blocks away, you and I decided to walk. I don't remember the particulars of what sent us spiraling into an argument. Perhaps I raised the concern that you were smoking again or maybe I complained about the late hours you were keeping. What I can resurrect are the feelings of urgency and frustration in trying to extricate myself from the conflict. I felt cornered as you demanded we continue talking until we had reached a resolution. To me, resolving the problem seemed quite beyond our reach.

Still struggling, we arrived at Allie's. Before going inside, I raised my voice, believing that might jolt you into dropping the issue. But it did nothing of the sort. Instead, we attracted the attention of the family who was already inside.

Your transition from adolescence to adulthood was painful for both of us. I so wanted to be the kind of mother who could disagree without inciting conflict. I wanted to be accessible and supportive. I never wanted to be the target of your rebellion. I imagine you wanted to be different as well.

Years earlier, your Uncle Bruce told me I needed to stop arguing with you. I felt judged. Was I supposed to remain silent if I saw you doing things that could put you in harm's way? I loved you too much for that.

That last night, I had a little more success in avoiding a confrontation. We arrived home from a family dinner. You went upstairs to get ready for a night out with friends. Once finished with your shower, you called out to me from the bathroom to tell me that there was a "hole" in your leg. I found you wrapped in a towel, your hair still dripping wet. You lifted the towel to reveal a scrape on your leg that was maybe an inch in diameter. It didn't seem at all serious. I suggested that you apply some antibiotic ointment and a bandage, but you wanted me to do the honors. I was in the midst of something else and told you to take care of it. You followed me out of the bathroom, determined that I help you. I knew that this interaction could easily flare into an argument. I had a choice; I could refuse your request and end up in a battle or give in to what you asked.

I had you retrieve the first aid supplies and then patched you up. You were grateful, somehow seeing me tend to your wound as a sign of my love and involvement. In that moment, you needed mothering—not too much to ask for even at the age of twenty-two. Given the way the later hours of the evening played out, I too am grateful that you wanted my help and that I was able to provide that.

Perhaps all parent-child relationships are full of ups and downs, contradictions that propel us through life. Yours and mine just seemed to hit extremes.

*   *   *   *   *

God, teach us to treat our families with more respect, and to hear their opinions without trying so hard to prove we are right.
Rebecca, 1996

Thirty Four

Send forth Your light and Your truth —
They will guide me.
    Psalm 43:3

I continue to gaze at the night sky, cradled by a force that is so much greater than me...

    I am fidgety and apprehensive at the prospect of Mothers' Day. The words alone, *Mothers' Day*, seem cruel. So, when Bob suggests that we leave town, I latch on to this ready-made escape. We settle on Big Sur, but as we head north, I remember that Big Sur was always one of your favorite haunts. How did I manage to overlook this in planning the trip? Big Sur is not going to help me avoid my grief. Instead, it is likely to submerge me in yet more memories and sadness.

    At eleven, you loved anything that involved being outdoors. Big Sur was appealing with its dense forests, trails that weaved up the mountains, and sunlight that threaded in through the thick foliage of the towering redwoods. After dusk, you and Jake would ask for a nighttime walk, leading the way for Dad and me with your flashlights illuminating our path.

Bob's voice draws me back. "I thought we'd have the chance to go on family trips, to take Becky's children fishing and hiking. I miss her."

I stare out the window as he navigates the twists and turns of Highway 1. Is this how the entire weekend is going to be, with both of us so keenly aware of your absence?

*   *   *   *   *

That last camping trip before your dad and I divorced filled me with anxiety. Tensions between us had reached such a pitch that I feared our marriage was coming to an end. I hated the thought that this might be our final trip together as a family. At eleven and a half, you were well aware of the strain between your father and me.

Leaving Dad and Jake behind at the campsite, you and I set off on a walk. You quizzed me about whether Dad and I were getting divorced. I told you that we were trying to work things out, but you were not appeased.

One month later, your father announced to me that he was leaving the marriage. I felt as though my world was coming to an end. When your father told you and your brother about his decision to move out, Jake flared in anger, crying and then hitting Dad. Jake's rage was fueled by the fact that your father had promised the two of you that we would never get divorced. I remember you being subdued and sad as you clung to me. It was only later that your anger and frustration surfaced. By then, Jake had retreated into silence; he spent the better part of the year depressed.

In time, all of us came to believe that the divorce had been necessary and was a better solution than Dad and I staying together. But in those first weeks, it seemed to me as if our world was tumbling down around us, and there was nothing we could do to stop it. I believe that at eleven and nine, you and your brother felt much the same way.

*   *   *   *   *

Bob takes the turnoff into the state park. The narrow road snakes through just as I remembered. The tires clack against the wood slated foot bridge. Below us is the stream that runs the length of the campground. Redwoods hug the road and form a tightly woven blanket that blocks out most of the summer sky. The sun peeks through the branches, sending thin shafts of light stretching down to the floor of the park. I think about the way the light used to play in your hair when you and I would take walks along this road. This place is filled with you, with us.

I see Jake and you crossing the wide stream, you hopping from rock to rock with graceful ease. Your urgings for your brother to follow along behind you are met with enthusiasm. I see the four of us hiking upstream, edging through narrow passages; huge, fallen boulders tower in high walls on either side. You are eager for us to push further than we have planned; we are in pursuit of the perfect swimming hole. Other images crowd in—the four of us snug in our sleeping bags, talking in hushed whispers before we drift off to sleep; you and Dad up early, long before Jake or I are ready to rise.

The next day, Bob and I take a drive up the coast toward Carmel. We spend hours exploring the nearby sea otter reserve. Late in the afternoon, we find an overlook that stands high above a sheltered cove. We watch in awe as three whales play and feed in the water below. The beauty and serenity of this place is amazing.

That evening, we stretch out in the darkness and stare up at the star-studded sky. I feel you holding me, pressing up against me. My tears are gentle. Bob reaches out and takes my hand. I continue to gaze at the night sky, cradled by a force that is so much greater than me. I find comfort here and in my memories of you. Though you have died, I know that I am still your mother. That is to be celebrated. I am more at peace than I have been in a long while.

My dread of Mothers' Day has eased. Bob and I decide to return home in time to spend the holiday with Grandma and Grandpa. Mothers' Day no longer seems like something from which I need to hide.

*   *   *   *   *

Mom,

Happy Mother's Day! I love you so much! I know at times we have hit a few bumps but I really love you and I am thankful you are my mom!

Love,

—Becky, 1996

Thirty Five

All children, except one, grow up.
    J. M. Barrie, Peter Pan

I am a soldier preparing for battle...

June brings with it Tahli's high school graduation. The prospect of sitting in the same bleachers where I watched you accept your high school diploma leaves me apprehensive. The day is sure to be bittersweet.

The night before graduation, Bob works late. I arrive home to an empty house that is weighted down with silence. Taking refuge in your room, I curl up on your bed and draw your pillow close. How I wish that I was holding you instead.

When the tears come, I drive to Aunt Allie's house. I find Jayni and Zach in the living room. Not wanting your cousins to see me this upset, I retreat to my sister's room at the back of the house. Allie follows after me and watches as I pace back and forth.

When she asks me what is wrong, I tell her that I want you back. She presses a fistful of tissues into my hand.

"Why wasn't it me instead?" I choke out. "I've had fifty

years; Becky only had twenty two." I reach the end of the room and spin around to retrace my steps. "This wasn't supposed to happen. I was supposed to protect her, keep her safe." A deep, shaky breath. "Why didn't I stop her from going out that night?" I plead. "I could have told her not to go."

"She wouldn't have listened." Allie tells me. "You know that. Becky wasn't a little girl; she was already grown. It was her decision to go out."

"I could have blocked the door."

By now, Allie is crying as well. "And what would Becca have done then?"

I shrug and shake my head, then plop down on the mattress.

"She would have argued with you, made you move out of the way. There wasn't anything you could have done. Besides, Becky didn't know there was going to be a crash. She didn't know she was going to die; no one knew that."

"Becky and I both knew it was coming."

Allie sidles in next to me. "You can't tear yourself apart with all the what-ifs. Those won't bring Becky back. You were a good mother; you loved her." By now, her arm is around my shoulder. Is she going to respond to my comment that you and I both anticipated your death?

We sit with one another for a while longer until the doorbell rings. Allie explains that she and some friends have plans to attend a teacher appreciation party, but she offers to stay with me instead.

"No, you go," I tell her. "I'll be all right."

Despite her protests, I remain steadfast. She disappears to greet her friends, but soon resurfaces to ask when Bob will be arriving home. When I tell her that he'll be there in an hour, she reminds me that Zach and Jayni are both around if I need them.

"I'll be okay," I assure her.

When she goes, your cousins come to check on me. They

settle on the bed; we talk about their day, their summer plans, you.

Jayni eventually leaves to meet up with a friend, but Zach stays for a long time. He holds me and tells me how sorry he is that you have died

*   *   *   *   *

On the day of graduation, I am a soldier preparing for battle, my weapons a pair of sunglasses to hide my red and swollen eyes and a thick wad of tissues that I've shoved into my pocket to deal with the inevitable tears. The truth is that everyone in the family is wrestling with your absence. Your aunts are weepy; Grandma and Grandpa are quiet; even your cousins are subdued.

As the processional begins, the graduates file on to the field wearing squared-off black caps and gowns that billow with each step. I scan the throng for a glimpse of Tahli. I think about how excited you would be about her graduating. At your own commencement, you were triumphant and jubilant as you marched across the field.

The day is warmer than usual. Nearby, women use folded programs to fan themselves.

"There she is," I hear Bria say. I follow the line of her outstretched arm.

The sequence of events is predictable—the mandatory singing of the National Anthem followed by speeches, the presentation of awards, and then, what we have all come for, the handing out of diplomas.

As the ceremony comes to a close, the graduates toss their caps overhead. We cheer along with the other spectators and then begin the slow descent to the field.

Five years ago, you were one of the graduates being celebrated. I looked down at you from the bleachers. You were beaming, so excited and full of anticipation at what lay ahead. I love the photo from that day of you holding a spray of sunflowers. Your cousins surround you, and all of you are smiling; but yours is the face that is filled with relief and pride. What an incredible moment!

Now, I've made it through Tahli's graduation. Next week, Aaron graduates from UC Davis. Everyone in the family will be there. Though pleased for him, I dread having to make it through another graduation. Do I have that much strength and resolve? Besides, Tommie's arraignment is coming up. I will have to choose between that and the graduation. It seems I lose either way.

*   *   *   *   *

Bob and I settle on staying behind in Ventura, feeling a responsibility to be at the arraignment. Arriving early at the Government Center, we cross the quad to the courthouse and line up behind others who are waiting to go through security. Who are all these people—victims of crime, perpetrators, attorneys? Though I've worked at this complex for years, today this place intimidates me. It doesn't matter that I am the psychologist for Probation and the Juvenile Superior Court; it doesn't matter that I am in court at least once each week. Today I am a parent who has lost her child to a drunk driver. This very familiar place has become foreign, leaving me to feel estranged and uncomfortable.

We take the elevator to the fourth floor, then walk hand in hand to the courtroom. Bob pushes open the large, double doors and motions me inside. After finding seats toward the rear of the room, we wait for the case to be called. As I scan the other faces, I wonder whether any of these people are related to Mike or Tim. None of these faces seem quite as sad as mine. *Perhaps the other families are not here*, I reason. Later, we learn that none of the other families have attended the arraignment.

Tommie waits until the last possible moment to enter the

courtroom. Sickened at the sight of him, I push down the rising nausea. Still, I can't look away. I stare as he makes his way to the front of the room. I study his face, the movement of his body. Am I searching for some sign of remorse?

What's going through his mind? What is he feeling? His presentation tells me nothing. His expression is flat, stoic. And his physical image is something that will stay with me for a long time—dark shoes and slacks, powder blue button-down shirt, wavy blonde hair that reaches halfway down his neck. There is no significant weight loss, no sickly pallor to his skin. I had expected profound changes, some visual sign of the trauma he has gone through. Odd, how he seems so unscathed, except for a slight limp and the fact that he is walking with a cane.

He takes a seat next to a woman whom I recognize as his mother. Bob whispers to me that he hopes our presence will leave Tommie feeling uncomfortable and make him think about the damage his carelessness has caused, but I see no indication of this.

Nothing substantial happens at court. The case is continued; we are frustrated and spent. That evening, I call the family. They're at dinner celebrating Aaron's graduation. Bob and I sing a congratulatory song to him and then talk with each family member, giving them the update about court. We underplay how upsetting it has been to see Tommie.

Later on, I go into your room and look at the photos on your shelves. I run my finger over your image and tell you that I love you. Do you hear me, Rebecca? Tonight, there is no answer.

*　　*　　*　　*　　*

My cousin Tahli is six; she is nice and she is very cute. I love her a lot; we are like sisters because we do everything together. I wish Tahli was my sister because I could see her a lot. I love to do her hair. I hope I can babysit her sometime. We say the same things because Tahli copies me with everything I do. If I can't have a sister it is nice that I have Tahli because we can be like sisters. I like it when we call each other sister because I like that.

Rebecca, January 21, 1991

Thirty Six

A dream that has not been interpreted is like a letter that has not been opened.
   Talmud, Berachot 55a

Peace abide you and keep you, my child...

Waking, sleeping, it doesn't matter what state I'm in; you are on my mind. I dream that you and your brother are playing basketball with your stepsiblings. You're laughing and charging around the court, tossing the ball at the hoop without any concern about scoring points. Enjoying the game is all that matters. You're smiling, and your long hair is streaming behind you like a glossy ribbon.

In another dream I see you and Jacob walking into the house after having been away for many days. Your expressions change to sadness as I explain that your grandfather has died. Jake is tearful. You ask which of Grandpa's belongings we will be able to keep.

"We won't take any of his things right away," I answer, but you continue on with more questions.

"Grandma will hold on to Grandpa's things," I explain.

"Eventually, if there are items she doesn't want, then we'll divide those up within the family."

You seem edgy and irritable, so I tread with care. Though dreaming, I am aware that you have preceded all of us in death. When I awaken, it is with profound sorrow. You were supposed to have lived longer than your grandparents, longer than your father or me.

The third dream deals with me giving birth. I observe this as though I am out of my body. I see the baby crowning, then being pushed into the world. When I realize that the infant is a girl, I conclude that it must be you. Later, I change my mind and reason that since you came into my life through adoption, the baby must be Jacob. Though still asleep, I try to reconcile the inconsistencies by altering the dream and changing the baby's gender from female to male.

Days go by before I share this dream with Aunt Leslie. She suggests that the baby in the dream represents you rather than your brother and asks me to think about the image of giving birth in a symbolic way. She tells me that she has always believed that you and I were meant to be together and points out that there are different ways of giving life and becoming a family. Her interpretation of the dream is reassuring.

In a fourth dream, I see myself on a bus with many children. We are on our way to some sort of Jewish lecture or celebration. Although the driver of the bus physically reminds me of an old friend of mine, I am certain that the driver is actually Bob. Looking out the window, I notice masses of people lining the road. They are making the same trip that we are. Some of them travel on foot, while others by car. I wonder if this is some sort of pilgrimage. When we stop, I realize that one of the children is missing, a young girl of five or six. Her name is Amy. Yes, I know. It's probably no coincidence that that is your middle name.

I beg Bob to stop the bus so that I can find the girl, but he refuses. He tells me that I can look for her once we reach the top of a long grade. He explains that if he stops now, we will lose momentum and reminds me that it was *my* job to keep Amy safe; it's *his* job to drive the bus. I can't change his mind. Once over the crest of the hill, he pulls on to the shoulder. I rush out the door and search for Amy, but there are so many obstacles. Upon awakening, I'm unable to recall the specifics of these.

What I do remember from the dream is that there are many people walking on the side of the road, but they are traveling in the opposite direction from me. Some nod and make eye contact with me. An older man tells me that he has been moved by my words. At first, I don't know what he's talking about, but then realize that he's referring to what I wrote for your funeral. I steel myself against the rising emotion because I have to stay focused on finding Amy. I worry that she's been hurt or taken against her will.

The girl in the dream is you; I'm sure of that. Her physical appearance reminds me of you at that age. I believe that the dream has to do with my desire to keep you safe and to hold on to my memories of you. So many people tell me that I must move on and not live in the past. What they don't understand is that I don't want to do that if it means letting go of you.

The dreams stay with me over the next few days. Even though you have died, I continue to be haunted by the conviction that it was my responsibility to keep you safe. With you, Rebecca, that duty went beyond the usual commitment a parent makes to a child. You were my first; that, along with the fact that you were adopted, heightened my obligation. I willingly took on the commitments and promises your birth mother relinquished. I know that giving you up must have been one of the most difficult things she ever had to do, but I also know how much pain that relinquishment brought to you. Convinced that I needed to make up for those things, I strove to be the perfect mother. Your death leaves me convinced I have failed. My commitment was to both you and your birth mother. Is she aware of your death? Has she kept tabs of your life and tracked your achievements? What must it be like for her to have let go of you as an infant and now once again as a young woman?

In the last dream, I frantically search for you, but never find you. Is this a statement about my inability to protect you from the ultimate danger? I think about you every day. I want to know how you are, where you are. What are you thinking and feeling? Despite my strong belief in an afterlife, I can't help but worry about your well-being. Some things do not change.

Peace abide you and keep you, my child.

*   *   *   *   *

Reanne Singer

The Dancer I Should Have Been

The dancer I should have been
Has long elegant legs.
She has a tall, thin body that moves like the wind.
The dancer I should have been
Moves perfectly to the beat of the music.
She can easily learn a dance in a single class.
She never misses a class
And she is always on time.
The dancer I should have been says,
"I can't possibly eat an ice cream sundae.
I will be too fat to dance and no one will like me."
The dancer I should have been
Would be famous and dancing with the Joffrey Ballet.
She has so many invitations to dance
With different companies around the world
That she has lost track.
All she ever does is
Go to class and obsess about her diet.
The dancer I should have been
Wishes she were more like me.
Having fun with her friends,
Hanging out at the beach.
And having enough time to do well in school.
        Rebecca, May 6, 1996

Thirty Seven

It is frightfully difficult to know much about the fairies, and almost the only thing for certain is that there are fairies wherever there are children.

J. M. Barrie, Peter Pan

Blessings continue on...

It's like clockwork; the end of summer arrives, and Bob is intent on making his yearly trek to Mammoth. Given that there is no way to dissuade him, I agree to go with. We are up before dawn to finish the last of our preparations. As Bob locks up the house, I am filled with panic at the thought of going away and leaving you behind. In an attempt to ease my pain, Bob reminds me that you're all right and not limited to only being in this place.

Six hours to Mammoth; the drive across the Mojave provides plenty of opportunity for reflection. Mile after mile of boring desert, the bland stretches of barren landscape broken up by the occasional cactus and tumbleweed. The tiny towns that dot the scorched earth remind me of when I was a little girl and traveling with the family. As we would approach one of these outposts, my father would have us hold our breath until we had passed the last building, an endeavor that took only a few seconds. Breezing through town, we would contain our giggles; as we finally inhaled, we would sputter forth with proud chortles.

Every once in awhile, the highway widens into three or four lanes. Impatient drivers pass as they zoom on to their destinations. Bob listens to music. I don't pay much attention to that or to his occasional attempts at conversation. I am lost in my own thoughts.

It is midafternoon when we climb the grade that leads to Mammoth. With the shift in elevation comes a change in scenery. The seemingly endless desert gives way to rolling hills. Off in the distance are the jagged mountains of the Sierras.

After setting up camp, we head out on an easy walk. At nine thousand feet, we don't want to attempt anything too strenuous on the first day. Our goal is only to stretch our legs and work out the kinks from the six-hour drive. When the sun dips behind the mountains, we head to the lodge in search of a comfortable place to pass the next hour.

Nestled at the base of mountains, Tamarack Lodge sits at the edge of the campground overlooking the lake. A few diehard fishermen gather their gear and walk back to their cabins and campsites with the day's bounty. The sky has turned from robin's egg blue to pitch black. The sudden drop in temperature heightens the appeal of the lodge for us.

As soon as I cross the threshold into the lobby, I am overcome with memories. You were only eight when your father and I took you and Jake cross-country skiing in these mountains. Surefooted and graceful, you easily navigated the snow-covered paths. Your brother had far more difficulty. Jake fell so many times that snow found its way inside his gloves, causing a mild case of frostbite. When the four of us took shelter in the lodge, you were charmed; you loved the large wood-paneled lounge with its overstuffed couches and chairs positioned around the stone fireplace. We peeled off soggy clothes and sipped hot chocolate while we thawed.

The flood of memories is more than I am prepared for. I withdraw to the campsite, but there is no escaping the past. The woods, the town, the lakes—all are filled with memories of you.

After dinner, Bob and I play backgammon and then read in the tent trailer. We go to bed early, spooning through much of the night to stay warm. I like burrowing into his bulk and feeling his warm breath on the back of my neck. I tell him about a trip years earlier with you, your brother, and father. We had gone to Tuolumne Meadows, high above Yosemite. The temperature had dropped to below freezing. All of us were nestled in sleeping bags and extra blankets. There was one extra bag remaining; you asked to use it, loving to nest beneath the weight of heavy covers. You were the only one in the family able to sleep comfortably that night. You weren't fazed by the thunderstorm or hail. Two sleeping bags and a blanket kept you toasty, allowing you to dream while your father, Jake, and I huddled together, shivering, waiting for morning to arrive. When the sun rose, you were thrilled to find that the night's rain lay frozen in pools on the ground. You urged us to hike through the rain-soaked meadows to long ago abandoned cabins.

The memories work like a salve that covers a raw wound and allows some healing.

The trip to Mammoth presents me with other gifts. It gives Bob and me space and time to grieve, as well as time to spend with one another. As we trek through the mountains, we come upon an amazing array of dragonflies and butterflies. We explore the trails that crisscross through the rugged terrain with these creatures accompanying us, dancing in circles and figure eights. Careening in front of us, around us, it's as if they are insisting that we take notice. Of course, their presence makes us think of you.

By the end of the trip, I am more at ease with your death and ready to return home. The ride home is long and tedious. The desolate landscape of the Mojave stands in stark contrast to the lush forests of Mammoth. Soon bored with the lack of appealing scenery, I pick up pencil and paper and sketch Bob's profile.

Forty minutes later, I put aside the drawing and look out the window. We are still in the midst of the desert; the long thin road reaches far off into the distance. My back is stiff, my legs restless. Fidgeting, I search for a more comfortable position. I glance out the window again and notice a wide expanse of clouds off to the right, their shape that of an immense dragonfly. Atop the cotton-fluff creature sits a young girl with long hair flowing behind her. *Perhaps it's just my imagination*, I reason. You know how you can see almost anything in the clouds. The wind softens the edges of the image before the dragonfly fades away.

I stare out the other window and spy a second dragonfly in the clouds. As with the first, a girl is perched on top.

"Look at the cloud," I say to Bob, careful not to tell him what it is I have seen.

He tells me that it looks like a girl riding on a dragonfly.

When I mention the first cloud, he is not surprised. He drives on and watches the sky for more signs of you.

Construction on Highway 395 causes traffic to slow to 20 mph. I am frustrated with the delay, but when a dragonfly hovers alongside our car and keeps pace with us, my annoyance gives way to wonder. Yet another gift to be found out here in the stark Mojave.

Dragonflies remain a presence for us even after we return home. The following night, we go to Aunt Allie's for dinner. I tell her about the clouds in the desert and how they took on the shape of dragonflies. She reports that while we were out of town, five dragonflies circled around her, staying nearby for a long time. Over the next days, when Bob and I walk through the neighborhood or down by the beach, dragonflies dance just inches from our faces and then weave a path around us. Even when we go to a local store for a few grocery items, there is a dragonfly that swooshes in through the open door and hovers by us as we stand in line at the checkout counter. I can't explain these experiences except to say that we know you are with us, Rebecca.

*　　*　　*　　*　　*

You loved to go into the wilderness. Hiking, camping, swimming—it didn't matter the activity, as long as you were in nature. One day, not too long ago, you and your friends went hiking in the mountains above Ojai. You ended the day with a soak in the natural hot pools. When you arrived home, your clothes were covered in dust and your hair reeked of sulfur. Your silver butterfly necklace was blackened from the minerals in the water. But you weren't bothered; instead, you were enthused about the adventure. A warm shower and shampoo restored the shine to your hair, and a wipe of a rag dipped in tarnish remover renewed the butterfly's sparkle.

Though typically burdened and stressed by your studies at the local college, on this particular day you were relaxed and full of joy. There was no indication of the pressures you felt from school or the questions you had about your direction in life. There was only this day, the inviting weather, and your outing with friends. Your energy was contagious. I was struck by the fact that you were no longer a teenager but a beautiful young woman whose life was so full of possibilities.

Since your death, I find comfort in wearing your necklaces, always keeping your tiny silver heart around my neck and alternating back and forth between the butterfly and the dragonfly charms. I fall asleep at night, holding the figures between my fingers, deluding myself into believing that it is you instead I am touching. I settle into the *Papasan* chair in your room and think about you curled up in this same space. I read your diary, drink in every word as though there is sustenance to be found here. So many references to butterflies, dragonflies, and fairies in your writings. Your bookshelf is lined with silver, ceramic, and glass renditions.

How is it that I didn't realize how important these creatures were to you when you were alive? Was I not paying close enough attention? Were you keeping this fascination to yourself? How I wish that you had talked to me about these things. How I wish that I had thought to ask! Do you know that I'm paying attention now, my love? I try to understand what you were thinking, what was in your heart a few months ago. I talk with others about the symbolism of dragonflies, fairies, and butterflies. I study. I learn. Your dragonflies, fairies, and butterflies have become a bridge that connects me to you.

The butterfly represents change, metamorphosis. I wonder about the changes that happen after we die. Do we hold on to some form of consciousness? And if so, does that mean that you can still see me, hear me? One thought leaves; two others come in its stead. Are you aware of my sadness? Are you lonely? God, I hope not. I want you to be safe, happy. I want you to look forward, to move on. I'm so impatient and frustrated at not having answers to my questions.

Fairies encapsulate the concept of magic, but with a spiritual overlay. I learn that they symbolize hope and a granting of wishes; they are an ethereal representation of nature. I also read that they symbolize independence of the female spirit. I can understand how you would have been captivated by all of this.

In recent weeks, Bob and I attended a conference on disaster training. I was apprehensive as the lecture turned to the topic of trauma, fearing that it would trigger thoughts about your death. During a break, I spoke with the instructor and told her about the crash that had taken your life. My purpose in telling her was to explain that I might need to take some breaks during the day in order to take care of myself. She was kind and sympathetic. Her gaze drifted to the dragonfly necklace that I was wearing. When she commented on it, I explained that it had been yours. She talked to me about a friend of hers who had lost a son a few years earlier. She said that her friend had found comfort in collecting dragonflies. She then asked if she might send me a book she thought I would like. I readily accepted.

The book arrived a few weeks later with a note indicating that dragonflies are thought to represent movement toward light or God. Some say that the symbol of the dragonfly has to do with going beyond the confines of this realm to a more spiritual dimension. It's not surprising that you would be drawn to such an image. The metamorphosis of the butterfly and the magic and spirituality tied up in the literature about fairies all fit with how I see you, Rebecca. Blessings continue on.

*   *   *   *   *

Earth...A Gift From God

Earth
A sphere
Turning, spinning through space
Created by God.

Waters surging, tumbling
Full of life
Mountains reaching high
To the end of the Universe

Vast forests
Stretching for an eternity
Beautiful creatures
Roaming about

A gift from God
To be cherished and protected
Preserving its goodness
A shelter for all
With guidance from God
        Rebecca, 1996

Thirty Eight

We live in all we seek....Holiness lies spread and borne over the surface of time and stuff like color.
    Annie Dillard, For the Time Being

Their eyes are wide as I tell them about the times when I have felt your presence...

Hosting a family barbeque over Labor Day weekend seems like an opportunity to make it through without too much angst. After all, there aren't a lot of emotional overtones and memories associated with Labor Day.

It is early evening, and some of us congregate in the kitchen as we finish up the food preparation. Les and Bruce talk with Grandma and Grandpa on the back patio while Bob mans the grill. Once everything is taken care of in the kitchen, I go out back and sit in the hammock. Tahli and Bria slide in next to me; the woven netting sags with our weight. With long legs dangling to the ground, Tahli and Bria rock us back and forth. Zachary and Jayni settle nearby on the grass. Memories trickle in—family dinners, overnights, play dates with your cousins. Everyone is grown up now; I miss the energy of all the young children. Still, it feels good to be surrounded by your cousins.

"What do you think happens after somebody dies?" Bria asks.

I talk with her about my experiences of you since your death. Your other cousins listen closely. Their eyes are wide as I tell them about the times when I have felt your presence, heard you, seen you. Jayni asks for more details, so I tell her about the Tarot card reading with Ron.

Bria turns to face me. "And you wanted me to house-sit when you went to Mammoth?" She is incredulous. "I wouldn't want to be alone in your house."

Her comment surprises me. I wouldn't have expected that she would be afraid of anything having to do with you.

"Becca would never hurt you," I tell her.

"I know that, but it would just be too weird."

"Tell us more about what you saw and heard," Jayni says. "I want to know what it was like."

She probes for details, approaching the topic as though she's a scientist who is trying to determine what is real and what isn't. I imagine that my experiences of you challenge the bounds of her usual reality. It strikes me that there is quite a difference between the two sisters; Jayni wants the concrete data while Bria is caught up in what she sees as the strangeness of what I am describing.

Tahli and Zach reveal that they, too, have seen you and heard you since your death. Zach talks about seeing more than the usual number of dragonflies and butterflies. Both he and Tahli see peripheral movements that they attribute to you. I would have expected Zachary's response to be more like Bria's; instead he seems much more aligned with his sister, Tahli. As I study his lanky frame and the face that is turning from boy to man, I am pleased that he can acknowledge having had these encounters with you.

"I worry that Becky was afraid when the crash

happened," Tahli confides, her voice trembling with emotion. "I hate to think that she knew she was going to die. What if she was in pain? I don't want it to have hurt."

"I don't either." I wrap her in a firm hug. "I think it happened quickly. I like to believe that if Becca knew what was happening, it was only for a moment. Then it was over."

I don't share with her that I, too, am tormented with the thought of you having had even a moment's awareness of what was happening that night. Tahli has struggled with so much sadness and worry since your death. I don't want to add to that.

When I tell Aunt Leslie about the conversation with the cousins, she indicates that she continues to see you and feel you as well. There was one day not too long ago when she and Tahli were at home. Tahli was reading in the living room, clad in one of your sweaters, the gray fuzzy one you liked so much. Les was putting on her makeup in the back of the house when she caught a glimpse of a girl in the gray sweater. It was logical for her to assume that the girl was Tahli, but when Les turned to get a better look, no one was there. Hurrying out to the living room, she found Tahli still on the couch engrossed in her book. Aunt Leslie insists that it was you she saw that morning.

The truth is what we know in our hearts to be real.

* * * * *

My friend and cousin spending time with you;
In spring and summer, autumn, winter, too.
You are always there when I need to talk;
It never matters the time on the clock.
The things we share, the one with the other;
Oh gosh, there are so many to cover.
From laughs to tears, and the stories we share;
I always know you will be the one to care.
Relying on you, always a best friend;
We work to stay like this until the end.
         Rebecca, October 7, 1997

Thirty Nine

Life makes warriors of us all. To emerge the victors, we must arm ourselves with the most potent of weapons. That weapon is prayer.
        Rebbe Nachman of Breslov

Grief descends again with unabashed force...

Another in a series of court proceedings finds Tommie entering a plea of "not guilty". I am furious. It would be so much easier on us if he would just admit to what he has done. The date for the preliminary hearing is set. This is going to be a long, drawn-out process.

Later in the afternoon when I am back at work, one of my coworkers stops by my office and informs me that in recent weeks her twenty-three-year-old stepdaughter has seen Tommie at a local restaurant. Cindy tells me that Tommie was drinking before getting behind the wheel of a car and driving. What *chutzpah*! Tommie kills three people, goes to court and pleads not guilty, and then has the gall to drink and drive again. What in the hell is it going to take for him to recognize that he has a problem? Is he that lacking in awareness or is he actually cold and uncaring? I once believed that he deserved compassion and help. Now, I'm convinced that he should face the harshest punishment possible.

The pain doesn't stop. We are coming up on the end of summer, which means that the anniversary of your death is only a few months away. Your father and I need to decide on a headstone for your grave. God, I don't want to do this. Grief descends again with unabashed force.

I need the headstone to be perfect. It has to be a reflection of you and how we feel about you. But how do I accomplish that? Your father's suggestion that we have a dragonfly etched into the stone brings some relief. We go to the mortuary together, but I am disappointed with the images that are offered. I refuse one after the other of the stilted, cartoon-like drawings. But when I'm asked to describe what it is that I am looking for, I draw a blank. The anxiety and frustration return. Dad and I settle on me talking with a local stone-engraver I have heard about to see if he has any more suitable ideas.

Once home, I am quiet and preoccupied. It is late when I finally sleep, but that is only in fitful bursts. In the morning, I awaken tired and spent. At the office, I flit from one task to the next. I am restless and uncomfortable. My thoughts go to you, to the trial, to choosing a headstone.

I call Rabbi Lisa; she suggests that I go to the cemetery and look at the different stones. Perhaps that will give me more of an idea about what it is I want for you. I leave work early. After buying flowers, I drive to the cemetery. As I pass row after row of graves, I think about all the people who are buried here. There is so much loss in this one place.

After parking at the side of the road, I walk to your grave. I sit on the grass and talk with you about life and what's gone on for me and the family since your death. I set the flowers in the container at the head of your grave and then wander off to look at headstones.

How many times must I think it, say it? I don't want to do this; I don't want to choose your headstone! How am I supposed to accept that you are buried here and are never coming home to me? Cheated, that's how I feel. We should be out shopping together, having lunch downtown. Anything but this. I shouldn't have to pick a marker for your grave.

I drive to Temple with the hope of finding Rabbi Lisa there, but she's off-site. The empty sanctuary offers refuge. Along the walls are memorial plaques with the names of the deceased. I scan the names and pause at the empty space that will soon hold your name. I collapse onto one of the pews and surrender to the sadness. *No! Not my child!* The wave of grief drowns out all other thoughts, leaving only the sad and overwhelming loss.

When the wave finally begins to recede, I find myself praying. I ask for God's help in making it through another day of this pain. And I ask God to watch over you and keep you safe. I sit, quiet in the solitude of the dark sanctuary, in this cave where I have come in search of solace.

And then, in that moment of feeling so utterly alone, your voice floats in so soft I have to strain to hear it. *"It's all right, Mom. I'm here; it's all right."*

I nod in recognition. One breath and then another. "I can do this," I whisper. "I can make it through this day." All I have to do is breathe and listen.

Thank you for letting me know that you are safe, Rebecca. I need to pay attention to what you tell me. I need to believe it, to allow it to become a part of me. Is that why you're making contact, making your presence known? Is it to reassure me, to offer me a way through this grief? Perhaps so.

* * * * *

Of all the nice things someone could say about me I would most want them to say I am kind and have a good heart. This is more important than having lots of money, being pretty, or being better than anyone else. I feel good when people treat me kindly. I feel good when I am kind also. Some of my friends think it is important to be the best. They even lie to seem better than others. This makes it harder for me to trust them or to feel close to them. I think it is more important to be honest and kind. That way people trust you and know they can count on you. If more people acted this way we would have a wonderful world but too many people are worried about being better than others or having more than others do. That's not the way I am. I hope that people understand that about me.

Rebecca, December 15, 1994

Forty

I'm too young to know why it happened, and too old not to understand. Even though you are gone, your spirit remains with me, and your soul lends a helping hand. God grants me the strength to stand tall and remember you always, so I still have a way to say I love you.

> Ariana Rothstein-Fisch and Vanessa Moran, Introduction
> to the Kaddish prayer

I find God, even in my solitude...

The High Holy Days are upon us. Past years have found me at Temple observing these times with the rest of the Jewish community, but this year, I am tempted to hide myself away and pretend that *Rosh Hashanah* and *Yom Kippur* don't exist.

It was only one year ago that you and I went to services together. You looked so sharp in your navy blue suit. Your hair had grown out from being cut the year before; I remember thinking how pretty it looked, hanging inches below your shoulders. Making our way from the parking lot through the foyer and into the sanctuary was like going through a maze. We skirted around the swarms of people who were greeting one another before the service. We did our share of shaking hands and kissing cheeks before finding our seats.

Once inside the sanctuary, you were all business as you pulled your *tallit* from its protective silk bag and then recited the traditional blessing before kissing one end of the prayer shawl and then the other. You wore a serious expression as you wrapped the *tallit* about your shoulders. I thought about the first time you wore that *tallit*, the day you became a *Bat Mitzvah*.

One memory links back to another and another. When you were an infant, I used to swaddle you in a baby blanket, your tiny body warm and safe against me. The actions of wrapping a child in a *tallit* and swaddling an infant are both about prayer and protection, about parenting and loving.

My thoughts shift to one year ago, to *Yom Kippur*. We were into the early afternoon portion of the service, and I was weary. I suggested that we take a break and leave for an hour before returning for *Yizkor* and the conclusion of the service. You objected, emphatic that taking leave would be disrespectful to God. Whether that was true or not wasn't the point. I wanted to support you in your observance. This seemed especially important given that in recent times you had wrestled with religion and how it fit into your life.

*   *   *   *   *

2004. You would be twenty-three, almost twenty-four. If you were still alive, you would be going with me to Temple for the High Holy Days. Nine months since your death—the amount of time it takes a life to grow inside a mother. Without you, I am hollowed out and empty. How can I possibly make it through the holidays?

Rosh Hashanah, the Jewish new year—a time for making resolutions, for starting anew. It marks the passage of time, something I don't want to confront. I have no desire to start a new year without you. That's like putting burning salt into a raw wound, the tender skin stinging with the bite, the flesh turning from pink to angry red. Why can't the year just fade away and not bombard me with all these firsts, all these milestones?

Yom Kippur looms ten days in the future after *Rosh Hashanah*. The holiest of days, *Yom Kippur* offers us the opportunity to make amends, to take stock of our actions, and to remember those who have passed on. So full of introspection and reckoning, the day is ominous, the anticipation of it oppressive. I picture this holy day as dark and dangerous, something that threatens to undo my fragile equilibrium. I don't want any part of *Rosh Hashanah*. I don't want to deal with *Yom Kippur* either.

I can't imagine tolerating the hours of prayer and observance involved in the holiday. I don't want to sit in the sanctuary with hundreds of other congregants and listen to the sermons, chant the prayers, or hear the traditional music. The worst part of the holidays will be the looks full of sympathy and pity from the other congregants. I can't handle any of it. Not now, not this year.

I search for answers and immerse myself in philosophical and religious writings. When I return to a book authored by Rabbi David Wolpe, his wisdom helps to move me forward. I reach some resolution as to how I will handle the holidays. In *Making Loss Matter*, he writes:

> The most famous prayer of Yom Kippur, Unetaneh Tokef, is a brutal recapitulation of the starkness of mortality. 'Who shall live and who shall die?' Because the prayer is recited but once a year, the congregation will inevitably look around for those who were present and praying last year but who are now gone. They too recited those words, not knowing that the coming year would claim them for death. The message is that mortality is wanton, capricious, death can strike anyone. It could strike me.

> *"The Unetaneh Tokef tells us that we do not have forever. Loss is not an incidental accompaniment to life, it is life's recurrent, urgent motif. Live with your eye on eternity and your foot fixed on the shifting sand, and forget neither one.*
>
> *Rabbi David Wolpe*

I don't take this prayer literally. I don't accept the idea that God decides our fate. I can't fathom a God who is responsible for robbing me of my child. If that was the case, I would have to renounce God. Thankfully, I am not faced with that decision. Instead, I seek comfort and reassurance from God.

The *Unetaneh Tokef* becomes for me a prayer to understand from a symbolic perspective. It transforms into a reminder of the tenuous and fragile quality of life. It is an invitation to treasure what we now have in the present.

Last *Yom Kippur*, I never would have believed that it would be my child who would be taken in the coming months, but this is the horror that has come to pass. The High Holidays take on new meaning and dimension. Like so many other days this year, they hold remembrances of you. They become trials I am determined to endure. Rabbi Wolpe invites us to accept that loss is a part of life, that we have to deal with this while also embracing the moment and living it to the best of our ability. Quite a challenge—to reconcile myself to the impermanence of life, cherishing what I have now, and not being consumed by fear and sadness of what the future holds.

In the end, I spend the holidays away from Temple. On *Yom Kippur*, I go to the cemetery and leave flowers at your grave. Bob and I recite the *Kaddish* prayer; we create a private, sacred moment of observance. Later in the day, I walk a long, lonesome stretch of beach and remember how I used to follow after you as you ran from one breakwater to the next. I find God, even in my solitude. In that, there is some easing of my grief. God will understand my departure from tradition this year. I hope you will as well.

*   *   *   *   *

Throughout my life, I have not always done a good job communicating with God, but I keep trying. When I pray I hope there is a God and that God hears me and takes my prayers into consideration. There can't be any total proof that God exists, but I think that praying is based on what you believe in your heart. Life is a very narrow bridge, and the most important thing is not to be afraid. Believing in God helps us maintain faith that things will work out, and it gives us the courage to persevere.
Rebecca, Confirmation, May 16, 1996

Forty One

The only truly dead are those who have been forgotten.
Jewish Proverb

Your voice echoes in my head...

When our friend, Lucianne, offers us the use of her timeshare in Hawaii, we gratefully accept. But after scheduling the trip, I am consumed with worries, fretting that going on this trip means leaving you behind and fearing that while we're away someone else in the family will die. Perhaps if I stay home, I can keep everyone safe. Prior to your death, I would have been concerned about my own safety, worrying that the plane would crash with me on it. That no longer frightens me. Now I reason that if I make it home, I will have more time with Jake and the rest of the family. But should I die, then I will be with you. That's nothing to fear.

Somehow, I manage to get to Hawaii. The amazing scenery on the Big Island makes it easy to contemplate a force greater than myself. It prompts me to consider the cycle of life and the interplay of God and man. Life throbs all around me— in the clear waters of the Pacific; in the lush growth of the tropics; and in the warm, humid air that is heavy with the scent of flowers, and salt water, and rich, dark earth.

As we trek around the island, we are delighted by the presence of dragonflies, numbers of them. Their translucent, paper-thin wings shimmer in the sunlight. Just like when we were in Mammoth, the dragonflies circle overhead and dance around us. We can't help but think of you and your profound love for these delicate creatures. Your precious dragonflies have come to symbolize a bridge between this life and what lies beyond. Their flight makes me think of the lifting of a soul from the physical body. I am reminded that love has no bounds. Though your life has ended, the essence of who you are and who you once were continues on.

A few days into the trip, I am startled by a nightmare. In the dream, I find myself in a rustic house with Bob. I soon discover your high school friend, Kristin, in the bathroom. When I ask her where you are, she tells me that you are not here. Dissatisfied, I question her again, but she only reiterates what she has already said. I turn away and catch sight of you stretched out in the bathtub. No longer aware of Kristin, I reason that she has left. I am horror stricken by your appearance. Your hair has been cropped short and dyed purple; you are easily fifty pounds overweight.

"Oh my God, Becky," I choke. "What have you done?"

"It's okay, Mom. Don't worry," you tell me.

"It's not okay. What have you done?" I demand.

"Everything's okay, Mom."

"No, it's not!" I repeat. "What have you done, Rebecca?"

You laugh, your voice a haunting cackle.

It is the middle of the night when I awaken, screaming and crying in terror. Bob holds me long after I quiet down. I am exhausted, but afraid to allow myself to fall back to sleep.

The images from the dream remain with me over the next three days. I talk with Bob about the dream and try to make sense of it, but nothing fits. He is unable to soothe me. I can't pull my thoughts away from the disturbing images.

On the third day, just before sunset, Bob and I set off for a walk. A mile out, his heel is hurting. I suggest that he remain behind at the boat dock while I continue on. He expresses concern about me walking this isolated stretch on my own, but I assure him that I'll be fine and promise to return soon.

The sun is low on the horizon and casts long shadows across my path. Wanting to get in as much exercise as possible before dark, I pick up my pace. Up ahead, I spot a coconut in the middle of the road. As I approach, I notice that one side of the coconut has been crushed, seemingly by the wheel of a car. My thoughts shift to you and the crash. I have the macabre image of your head being crushed like this when you were thrown from the truck.

Stop it, I tell myself, and try to push away the picture. *Bob told you about visiting Rebecca at the mortuary. He reassured you that aside from a few scrapes, Becca looked fine. She wasn't disfigured, didn't look like she'd been through a fatal trauma.*

The disturbing thoughts and questions persist.

And then I feel you, hear you. *"Don't worry, Mom. I'm okay. You have to stop doing this to yourself. I'm really okay. I love you."*

I answer in a solemn whisper. "Tell me about the crash, Rebecca. I need to know what happened that night."

Do I really want the answers? I question my own ability to handle what you might offer. But I need to know. Nothing can possibly be as terrible as the images I already have in my head.

"Were you scared, Rebecca? Were you hurt?"

You tell me you were only partially conscious when you were thrown from the truck. You were frightened and hurt, but that lasted less than ten seconds. Then you hit the rocks on the embankment and you were out of your body. You were confused for a short time. Then it was over.

"*Let it go, Mom. It's all over. You can't keep doing this to yourself. Let it go.*"

Amazed by the information you are giving me, I press on with even more questions.

"Are there things I could have done to keep you safe?" I say out loud.

Your voice echoes in my head. "*You did the best you could, Mom. I did the same. I wasn't supposed to die, but I did. I'm all right now. I'm going on with my journey. You need to do that as well. I love you.*"

I ask you what was happening right before the crash. You explain that the kids you were with had been drinking. The truck was filled with laughter and conversation. The others were joking around, and Tommie became distracted. He lost control of the truck.

Your presence fades, but you have brought me strength and comfort, Rebecca. As I retrace my steps back to where Bob is waiting, I wonder whether or not to tell him what has just happened. Will he understand or will this all seem too far-fetched and unbelievable?

Of course, when I talk with him, he is supportive. I am again reminded of how consistent he has been through this ordeal. Why would it be any other way now?

*   *   *   *   *

Wouldn't It Be Great If We Lived Without Pretense?

Imagine a world
Where we lived without pretense.

Young girls no longer wearing a mask of color,
Lips not requiring definition
With a smear of clownish red,
Eyes not hidden behind black lines,
True tones of a complexion
Without the cloud of powder.

People valued for who they are,
Not judged for who they seem to be.
No more coveting of body curves,
Or lean, lanky legs,
Finding beauty in varied shapes,
Accepting differences,
Treasuring ourselves.

Treating our bodies as holy,
Like sanctuaries to be cherished,
Not defacing them
With mutilating tattoos
Or self-punishing drugs and alcohol,
That remain for a lifetime.

Uncovering our individuality,
Unashamed to show
The core of our spirituality,
Treating others with respect and kindness,
Not just spouting the Golden Rule.

Why can't we live the way we were made?
Imagine a world where we lived in God's image.

Rebecca, November 11, 1997

Forty Two

Whoever destroys a single life is as guilty as though he had destroyed the entire world...
    Talmud, Sanhedrin 37a

My anger and sorrow continue...

It is only a few days after returning home that we receive a phone call from the D.A. indicating that Tommie has decided to plead guilty at his next court appearance. We are cautioned about the possibility of Tommie changing his plea, but are also assured that there will be no deals. Either Tommie pleads guilty or the D.A. takes him to trial. *At least there is that*, I think, finding the D.A.'s determination to see this through as reassuring. After all the months of waiting—the questions about Tommie's blood alcohol level, whether he would be charged with manslaughter, whether there would be any semblance of justice – and now we are here with somebody in a position of power standing beside us, assuring us.

An entourage of family and friends accompany us to court. It is my understanding that the parents of the other two who died along with you will not be here.

Bob and I are ushered into a private conference room where we are introduced by the D.A. to a highway patrol officer who was one of the first responders to the crash. The D.A. explains that this officer has taken the lead on the investigation. He is there in case Tommie changes his mind about the plea. The officer is prepared to testify about the investigation, Tommie seeming under the influence at the scene of the crash, the skid marks on the road, the state of the truck, the bodies of the victims and where they were found. The D.A. informs us that other witnesses are lined up as well— paramedics, highway patrol officers, the coroner, someone from the lab who did the toxicology report, lay people who happened on the scene.

Returning to the courtroom, I spot Tommie some distance away. He gives no indication of having noticed me. My stomach churns with nausea. The victim advocate escorts me out and down the long corridor to the restroom. I run cold water over my hands and splash my face that is now flushed and damp with sweat. A few deep breaths and I am ready to return.

As we walk in silence up the hallway, I see that Tommie is now sitting on a nearby bench, smiling and chatting with his attorney. I am appalled by his lack of distress. Is Tommie really so insensitive that he can present himself in such a free and easy manner? I want him to be consumed with pain and remorse. Maybe then, he will acknowledge the devastation and destruction he has brought upon us.

I keep my thoughts to myself and do not utter a word to the victim advocate. I pull open the heavy wooden door that opens to a short breezeway. We walk through another doorway and into the courtroom. Taking a seat between Grandpa and Bob, I am surrounded on all sides by familiar faces—Grandma, Les and Allie, Bruce, your dad and Cathy, your cousins, our friends. The victim advocate finds a seat in the row in front of us.

I peer around to see Tommie enter the room and take a seat in the back with his attorney. Tommie avoids looking in our direction. I find it so strange. He's been to our home many times, had dinner with us, visited. Today it's as if we don't even exist.

One case after the next is called. Are they ever going to call Tommie? Can't we get on with this? I feel like the air is being sucked out of the room. I reach for Grandpa and Bob and hold on tight. I study each of their hands. Bob's is full and padded, the skin the color of dark brown caramel. His calloused fingers are rough against mine. Grandpa's hand, though still large, is more bony than it used to be. The withered skin is pallid and dotted with liver spots and scratches and bruises that come so easily with age. I stare at the trail of blue veins and the way my much smaller hand is sheltered by his.

The bailiff calls out, "Tomas Edmundo Mercer, Jr."

I turn to see Tommie walk down the center aisle to the front of the room. He focuses straight ahead and guards against looking at us. He is clad in the same blue shirt he's worn to the previous hearings. *Is this the best he can manage? He's killed three of his friends and can't even wear another shirt to court?* Bizarre, the things that draw my attention and rage.

"Is that him?" Grandpa whispers, his voice gravelly.

I swallow hard and tell him yes.

There is a brief exchange between the judge and Tommie's attorney, but because of all the peripheral noise, it is impossible to make out what is said. A few feet away, an interpreter talks in Spanish with another defendant. I shoot her an annoyed look, but she doesn't react. I doubt whether she's even noticed me. Kim, a probation officer friend, tiptoes over and asks the interpreter to quiet down. The interpreter nods in apology.

The D.A. reads the charges. My breath catches as he says your name aloud. I clench Grandpa's hand, but then ease my grip as I remember his tender skin.

Tommie enters a plea of "no contest" rather than pleading guilty.

"What does that mean?" I ask Bob, but he doesn't answer. He holds up a hand to silence me so that he can hear the D.A.'s response, but the D.A. fails to raise an objection.

Bob shakes his head. "He's not admitting to anything."

I turn to my father who completed law school when I was a toddler, but never practiced. His face is pale, his ears red—a sure sign that he's upset. "Shit," he mutters. "Sonofabitch! Damn asshole!" Significant swearing coming from my dad.

Family and friends stir with hushed objections, except Grandma who is uncharacteristically quiet.

Bob and I meet with the district attorney, who explains that by entering this plea Tommie is making no attestation of guilt. Rather, it is a passive declaration. Tommie is not disputing the charges nor is he acknowledging them. He is not admitting any liability.

Bob's mouth is a tight gash. "Why aren't you pushing to go to trial like you promised?" he demands.

The D.A shakes his head and attempts to pacify us with words about how this will expedite things and spare us a painful trial. He explains that Tommie still has to pay a consequence for your death; that hasn't changed.

But the way I see it, we've been sold out, betrayed by the system for what, convenience? Perhaps I was a fool to believe that the district attorney was on our side. There is no justice, not for me. Tommie isn't taking responsibility for his actions. The plea of no contest is a slick maneuver by Tommie's attorney, it's purpose to protect Tommie in the event of a civil suit.

Tommie is allowed to return home for a few days before reporting to jail. Kim explains that he will be eligible for Work Furlough, a program which affords him the privilege of living in a county-run facility and working out in the community during the week. Chances are that he will spend very little time in jail. He will be on probation for three years. I'm stunned by the way everyone is taking care of him—the system, his family. They are enabling his alcoholic behaviour. His parents have secured one of the most successful criminal attorneys in town. For them, I guess it has paid off.

As for me, I am heartsick. There has been no word of apology, no offer of condolence, nothing to tell us that Tommie feels any remorse for what he has done.

Out in the hallway, we are met by Tommie's mother, who swallows me in an unwanted hug. Stiff and unyielding, I am unable to respond when she tells me how sorry she is about your death. Does she know that her son has not yet offered a single word of regret? I choke down my words. When she releases her hold on me, all I can do is turn away.

I picture her leaving the courthouse, her anxiety now replaced with relief. All the waiting and preparation for this day and now it is over. I, in contrast, have come to this day with my own anguish. None of that is diminished. Again I think about the unwanted hug from Tommie's mother. Perhaps it would have been more compassionate of me to return the embrace, to offer words of understanding. Like me, is she struggling with her own guilt? Does she question whether she could have done something to prevent this tragedy? Are we all that different from one another or only flip-sides of the same awful reality?

Still, what I come back to is that the court process has ended without any semblance of justice. You have died, and the man responsible for that has gotten away with only a mild reprimand. One mother has the privilege of taking her child home. Three others have had to bury theirs. My anger and sorrow continue.

*   *   *   *   *

Shattered Glass

Describe my grief
put it into words
so that others might understand
the depth of sorrow
that courses through me
blood in my veins

I know they will ask
they'll say it's my right
to share my pain
to ask for retribution
my answer straightforward, simple
justice

But there is no justice
nothing to soothe or console
nothing to repair the gaping wound
Justice! how absurd
they know this, and yet
still ask me to describe my grief

I reach
deep into my soul
search for words
to capture the pain
describe the nightmare
this cruel, unrelenting presence

The worst are those fleeting moments
when I forget that you have died
when I delude myself into thinking
that you'll return any time now
walk through the door, smiling, laughing
apologizing for such a prolonged absence

I startle with the memory
again hear the harsh pronouncement
you have died
my heartbeat quickens
a hollow emptiness
consumes me

They ask me to describe my grief
I tell them my life has turned to shattered glass
shards that cut, that wound
these lonely words echo
jar me once again
to face this harsh reality
                Reanne, June 4, 2004

*   *   *   *   *

Family
Security within the strong arms of a loved one
Supportive, loving
Comfort, safety
A shoulder to cry on

Rebecca, 1993

Forty Three

The room is full of you! — As I came in
And closed the door behind me, all at once
A something in the air, intangible,
Yet still with meaning, struck my senses sick!
> Edna St. Vincent Millay, "Interim", *Renascence and Other*
> *Poems*

We had quite a time of it…

Five more weeks and it will be one year since you died. Soon, we will unveil your headstone. I continue to grasp for the right arrangement of English and Hebrew words and the right drawing for the stone. A friend who is by trade a graphic designer, spends hours with me on the project, soothing me with her patience and understanding. Together, we arrive at a design that captures my feelings about you, Rebecca.

The stone engraver is an elderly man — short, slender, with wrinkled skin that is so translucent it seems that I can see every vein in his hands. Though much smaller in frame than your grandfather, his skin is similar, pale and thin like parchment.

I give him the drawing that I want transposed onto your headstone. As I hand over the paper, I find myself staring at the man's hands. I wonder what it must be like to be so old, so close to death himself, and to spend his time honing markers for those who have already died. Does he consider his own demise, wonder what will take him from this world? Has he already designed the stone that will sit atop his grave? So many morbid questions that I stop myself from speaking out loud.

He phones a week later to tell me that your headstone is complete. He asks that I come by his house to give final approval before he takes it to the cemetery. With only weeks standing between this moment and your *yahrtzeit*, this is not a task I can put off. It has to be done now.

Bob accompanies me. I have anticipated strong emotions and so am surprised when I see the stone and react with calm acceptance. The stone is as I intended, full of grace and beauty. It is an appropriate testament to you. Finally, this is a task I can lay to rest.

The irony is that with only one week until Halloween, there are tombstones and ghosts and goblins everywhere. With the fast approach of Halloween comes the realization that Grandma's birthday is only days away. Striving for some semblance of normalcy, I suggest that the family meet at our house for the celebration. After dinner, your cousin Zachary asks if he might rummage through the family room cabinets for a Halloween costume. He sifts through the array of treasures and surfaces in a shimmering green skirt and a tight fitting black top. Gaudy jewelry adorns his arms and neck. A brightly colored bandanna tied around his head tops off the outfit. Quite a look on his sixteen-year-old frame.

A rush of memories assaults me as I watch him parade around in clothing that you and your cousins once used for the holiday. Is no one else in the family affected by this? Don't they understand that since your death these clothes have not been touched?

Not wanting to put a damper on Zach's antics, I try to join in the family's laughter. In spite of my best efforts, my thoughts drift backward through time to past Halloweens.

*   *   *   *   *

When you were eight, you wore pink flannel long-johns and a matching hood with pointy ears for Halloween. Dark whiskers drawn across your cheeks left no question that you were a kitty-cat that evening. Jacob, at age six, was a skeleton, dressed in black pajamas with the outline of white bones embossed on the front and back. I think Aaron was a pirate and Tahli and Bria ballerinas. Jayni and Zach were still babies and too young for costumes. The family had congregated at Bruce and Leslie's house for dinner, makeup, and pictures.

Once we headed off through the neighborhood to trick-or-treat, you took the lead, directing your cousins to the various houses. As far as you were concerned, the night's jaunt was yours alone to oversee. The five of you moved *en masse* down the block, sometimes joining ranks with other trick-or-treaters, but then reconfiguring once again to form your own flock.

We covered lots of territory, walking a good number of blocks before piling into cars to drive to another part of town. More than two hours later, we ended up at our house, arms laden with pillowcases and shopping bags heaped full of sugary treats. Your faces were flushed with excitement. My voice was hoarse from cackling like a witch and howling at the moon.

After your cousins went home, you and Jake emptied your sacks of treats on the dining room table and began the very important task of sorting through the bounty and then negotiating trades until you were both content with your stash.

*   *   *   *   *

Recognizing my fondness for Halloween, a friend asks if I will be dressing in costume this year. I tell her that I'm not in the mood, that Halloween simply isn't the same without you. The holiday has lost its magic. Perhaps the best that I can do is to survive the day. I will answer the door and hand out treats to the neighborhood children. When Zach shows up at the house, draped in your clothing, I'll force a smile. And I will remember, Rebecca, that Halloween used to be one of our special times. We had so much fun slipping into our costumes and marching through the darkness where we were surrounded by ghosts, goblins, princesses, and monsters. We had quite a time of it, didn't we, my girl? I am glad for the memories. Maybe, just maybe, they will get me through yet another season without you.

*   *   *   *   *

I'm not sure if I'm going to dress up for Halloween. If I'm going to I'm either going to be a pirate or a clown with my best friend. I really like Halloween because I get to spend it with my cousins. Halloween is my favorite day of the year. I really like to go to people's houses to get candy and treats. I also like to stay home and give out candy to people who come trick or treating at our house.
Rebecca, October 13, 1993

Forty Four

When we think about those who have died, and try to understand their lives and teachings, we are permitting faith to shine through loss. Faith is not denying that the death was tragic, it is insisting that it can carry lessons, that it can bring meaning into the lives of those who remember.
        Rabbi David Wolpe, Making Loss Matter

I plod through the week leading up to Thanksgiving...

October gives way to November; what an ominous and dismal time of year this has become. A season that was filled with holidays and birthdays has become a time to dread. The days drag on and on as though we have entered a cruel time warp.

I plod through the week leading up to Thanksgiving and count down the days. On the Wednesday before Thanksgiving, I am consumed with the haunting thought that one year ago today would have been the final day remaining for any of us to be able to spend with you.

Grandma tells me that the year has gone by quickly for her; I feel as though I have slogged through it, much too aware of every moment. In recent weeks, I have been short-tempered, snapping at Bob and then offering up heartfelt apologies, only to sink back into irritability once again. Bob has been tolerant; he goes out of his way to avoid arguing with me. As we come to within hours of Thanksgiving, my bad temper gives way to sadness.

Allie has offered to host the holiday meal. That's good because I couldn't bear having it at our house this year. I no longer look forward to this day that used to bring me so much joy. Bob will bake some pies and a loaf of bread. That will be it. In the evening, we will go to your aunt's house. God only knows what we will do to make it through the rest of the day.

Thanksgiving unfolds with oppressive solemnity. I feel as though a heavy weight is pressing down on me, holding me in place. Bob and I go through the motions of breakfast, a walk with the dogs, and chores around the house. We call your brother in Australia. Jake reports that he is trying to stay busy and to get through the day as best he can. I worry about him being so far from home, picture him spending the day by himself. I am relieved when he tells me that he and his new friends are preparing a turkey dinner. What is even more reassuring is to hear that Jake has told these friends about your death. It is only another couple weeks until your brother's homecoming. Still, I wish that he were here with us today. Jake tells us that tomorrow he will go to a nearby temple to recite *Kaddish* for you. We, too, will be in temple with family and friends.

Later, Bob and I go to the cemetery to visit your grave. The grounds are decorated with American flags, balloons, and flowers. The gaudy presentation takes me aback. I feel as though I have happened on some morbid carnival rather than a burial site. I want this place to be more like what I have become accustomed to—quiet, low-key, even peaceful. But today, it reminds me of a poor rendition of a July 4th parade.

Bob parks the car near your grave. With flowers in hand,

we walk the few feet to where you are buried. The grass has filled in; the indentations that once attested to this being a new grave are no longer visible. But there is still no headstone. Though it has been one year since your death, we are postponing the unveiling until Jake's return home.

Bob wanders off to fill the metal flower container with water. I sit on the grass; my eyes fill with tears as I think about you here in this place. The words come more easily to me than they did a year ago. I have become accustomed to talking with you here. Before leaving, I set a small piece of blue ocean glass on your grave.

Arriving home, I wander through the house, unable to settle on any single activity. I attempt writing, but am too emotional to focus. I pick up a book, but reading takes too much concentration and patience. The words on the page make no sense; my mind is elsewhere. When Bob and I are in the same room, we are noticeably quiet, both absorbed in our own thoughts.

In the end, I land in the family room where I am drawn to the assortment of children's books I've saved from when you and Jake were small. I leaf through one book after the next, torturing myself with the memories. I hear your young voice and Jake's, both now only ghostly echoes. *Go Dog Go, Yertle the Turtle, Goodnight Moon....* I pick up one of the Shel Silverstein volumes and read page after page of the poetry you loved. I turn to *The Giving Tree* and find myself transported back. I am years younger with a preschooler and a toddler snuggled in against me.

I read the first words aloud. *If only this were real,* I think. If only you and Jake were nestled in with me, captivated by the familiar story. If I could take us back to those days, then as we moved forward in time I'd be wiser, more vigilant. I'd be able to undo the tragedy of twelve months ago. If only life and death were that simple.

It is late in the day, and I am still restless. I walk to Aunt

Allie's house where family and friends have begun to congregate. Bob chooses to remain at home a bit longer, preferring to lose himself in a televised football game.

As soon as I set foot in your aunt's house, I am even more aware of your absence. Not wanting to cry in front of people, I do my best to contain my emotions. Unable to calm down, I head out for a walk with Cousin Judie at my side. She listens to me, the two of us in tears as we walk the neighborhood arm in arm.

Upon our return, the house is even more full. The turkey is out of the oven, and there is lots of activity as the table is set and loaded with platters of food. Are we going to sit down and act as though this is a typical Thanksgiving?

As people gather at the table, Grandma stands and waits for the room to quiet. Is she going to offer a prayer or a toast? Neither one seems quite like her. Perhaps she will do the usual of inviting us each to share something we are thankful for.

Instead, she says, "This Thanksgiving, we're here without Rebecca. Thanksgiving has become a very sad day for our family."

I let out a deep sigh. *There it is*, I think, *the acknowledgement of your death.* My throat constricts; my eyes are wet. Still, this is so much better than pretending that Thanksgiving is the holiday it used to be.

"Our family has gone through a profound loss," Grandma continues. "All of us are left with so much sadness. But we are a family who can share memories and remember Becca when she was here with us. Let's take a moment for silent prayer before we eat."

I draw in a deep breath and close my eyes; the tears slide down my cheeks. I think about you and the time we had together. Now, I can say that I am thankful.

Thanksgiving has changed, but perhaps it is no longer a day to dread. Perhaps it is a time to acknowledge loss and also a time to come together with loved ones. It is a time to remember you.

*   *   *   *   *

I was a child
who was encouraged
to be myself.
At six months
I spoke my first word ...
cabbage.
I never once met
a person that had
that as their first word.
I live in two houses.
I'm one of three
and one of nine.
I have danced ballet
12 years of my life.

I swam in icy rivers
and climbed huge
mountains that
reached for the sky.
I only once
ate a piece of escargot,
dressed as a vampire.

On a dare
I asked an old lady
for a glass of milk.
I used to be scared
of the dark and
thought monsters
roamed under my
bed at night.
I am a girl with no appendix.
I have many
more adventures
yet to come.
     Rebecca, 1996

Forty Five

To everything there is a season and a time for every purpose under heaven.
Ecclesiastes 3:1

I smile through my tears and think that it isn't so bad that these seasons are filled with you...

The days following Thanksgiving become an elongated observance that consumes the majority of the weekend. Friday night brings with it *Shabbat* services and the recitation of *Kaddish*. It is freezing cold as we walk into Temple. I thread my arm through Bob's, searching for warmth and the resolve to walk inside the synagogue. I don't want to be here tonight. I don't want to have to stand and repeat the words of the Mourner's Prayer.

As we make our way into the lobby, I notice that there are fewer people present than usual. Most of the Temple's membership are at home tonight, devouring leftovers from their Thanksgiving feasts or simply taking advantage of the long weekend. The few people who are at the evening service know all too well what this day entails for us.

We are ushered into the sanctuary with heartfelt looks of sympathy and condolence. We ease down the length of wall that holds a great many memorial plaques and stop at the one that is now engraved with your name. I touch my hand to my lips and brush a fingertip across the cold, rough metal lettering of your name, then deposit a kiss on the plaque before finding my seat with family.

The service is more subdued than usual. Is this because there are so few people in attendance? To distract myself from what is coming, I run a finger back and forth across the weave of Bob's wool jacket. I am like a young child who finds consolation in the touch of a favorite stuffed animal or blanket.

The service continues. I trail along with the prayers but make no attempt to join in when the congregation sings. *Kaddish* approaches, and my apprehension grows.

Then Rabbi Lisa is reciting the names of those whose *yahrtzeit* is being observed tonight. I brace myself for what is to come.

And then it is upon me; the Rabbi looks in my direction and says, "Rebecca Amy Singer-Beilin."

Bob tightens his grip on my arm and nudges me to my feet. The rest of the family stands with us. There is no turning back. Voices rise around me, chanting the *Kaddish*. Their voices force me to say the words as well. I am light-headed. Bob's arm is around my waist, steadying me. Can he feel me tremble against him?

"*Yitgadal vityitkadash shemei raba.*"

I choke back the sobs.

The voices press on, insistent that we finish this task. They seem far off, thready. I move my lips to form the familiar sounds; the words come out in barely a whisper. I picture the words floating, hovering around me. Then they drift off, higher and higher, until they are out of my reach.

I anticipate some relief as we chant the last line of the prayer. "*Oseh shalom bimromav, hu yaaseh shalom aleinu veal kol*

Yisraeil, veimru: amein." But there is no relief, only exhaustion, a tiredness that I feel deep in my bones that leaves me limp and drained.

We take our seats. I am ready to go home. I want to lose myself in sleep.

*   *   *   *   *

In the days that follow, there is my birthday, then *Hanukah* and your birthday. Bob resists my attempt to ignore my birthday, telling me that being alive and turning another year older are still blessings. I acquiesce to having a quiet family dinner that has little to do with celebration and more to do with us just being together. It seems like enough for my fifty-second birthday.

Hanukah descends one week later. The last of the eight days of the holiday coincides with your birthday. In the past, *Hanukah* was met with eager anticipation. Potato *latkes* frying in the kitchen would fill the house with their heady aroma, making me hungry long before it was time to sit down for the meal. Colorfully wrapped gifts, the gleeful shouts of children during a game of *dreidle*, the lighting of the *menorah*, and singing traditional holiday songs were always things to look forward to. But this year is different; even *Hanukah* has lost its appeal. It has become a day to survive, not one to enjoy.

*   *   *   *   *

Hanukah eight years ago, the first of our guests arrived bringing with them handmade decorations. As more family and friends appeared, our home became filled with colorful, six-pointed stars, *menorahs*, and *dreidles*. We feasted on Grandpa's brisket that had been slow baked with dried fruit and onions, accompanied by *latkes* topped with sour cream and applesauce.

259

Once we'd had our fill, we retreated to the family room for our less than traditional white-elephant gift exchange. You took charge of writing numbers on small pieces of paper. Everyone at the party had brought a gift-wrapped item from home, the rule being that it had to be something they no longer wanted. The number on their scrap of paper would determine each guest's order in the white-elephant exchange. You marched around the room with great authority and instructed each person to reach into a basket and pull out a piece of paper.

When it was Jake's turn to select a gift, he scanned the assortment of packages that were arranged on the family room table and made his selection. As he opened his gift, you dissolved into uncontrollable giggles. Jake tossed the colored wrapping paper aside and surfaced with one of your bras. He held the padded cups overhead for all to see. Everyone joined in your laughter. You took your brother by the hand and led him to the garage where you cajoled him into donning the bra over his shirt. You both returned to the party looking very smug and pleased with yourselves. Jake modeled your bra; he strutted the length of the room as though he was completely at ease with the new look. Not too many people could have convinced a thirteen-year-old boy to endure such a scene, but you were quite capable of that.

This year, your cousins are determined to carry on the tradition of the gift exchange. I am not very enthusiastic, but in the end I agree. Maintaining our family traditions keeps you close. It reminds me of the good times. When it is my turn to select a gift, I think back to the fun-loving teenage girl who entertained us all that night eight years ago. I smile through my tears and think that it isn't so bad to have these seasons filled with you.

*   *   *   *   *

I'm so happy that Hanukah is coming soon. I can't wait to see what I got for my presents. I have so many things that I want so basically anything I get is okay. Plus if there is something I don't like I can exchange it for something else that I want. I have a feeling that I'm going to get a lot of things I want because I have already seen a few of my presents. Some of them are in my mom's closet and I walked into the kitchen and she was wrapping some presents, so I saw some of them. Well, I can't wait. Just a few more days to go!

Rebecca, December 5, 1993

Forty Six

There is strong shadow where there is much light.
Johann Wolfgang von Goeth

I can't help but think that I want both of you here with me…

Jake's homecoming arrives in slow motion, like heavy molasses that lingers in the pouring. I move from one set of preparations to the next. I make sure that Jake's room is dusted and aired out with clean sheets on the bed. I straighten the house, as if your brother would even notice if things were in disarray. I call the rest of the family and remind them that they are expected here for dinner tomorrow night. Grandma asks if I'm sure that Jake will be up to company after the long flight home. I assure her that I have already cleared the plans with him and that he's looking forward to seeing everyone. At the market, I fill my basket with Jake's favorite foods—ice cream, salmon, and the makings for teriyaki turkey burgers. Aunt Allie has brought over bright yellow butcher paper so that I can make a welcome home banner. That, and assorted balloons, will decorate the front porch.

I am eager to hear about Jake's travels and to see how he

has changed. I wonder if he will look different, sound older, be more mature. Will he notice the differences in me, the wrinkles around my eyes and the profusion of gray strands that now twine through my hair?

Jake will be seventeen hours in the air, which translates into endless hours of me praying for his safe return. I run through the calculations in my head, backtracking from the hour of his arrival to the time of departure, figuring in the time difference between California and Australia, and then arriving at the minute that he will be taking off. I picture the way the sky will look in Australia, at what point during the flight it will be daylight, nightfall. Over the next day, I plot out where on the globe he will be at any given moment, following the course of his journey as he makes his way back to me.

*   *   *   *   *

Eighteen months before, when you heard that your brother was going abroad for his senior year, you insisted that you would visit him in Australia. You didn't have any idea how you were going to come up with the money for the flight, but that did not stop you from making plans.

It seemed to me that you were both proud and jealous of him, not unlike the way you had felt about him for most of your life. You were just under two-and-a-half when Jake was born. I figured that I had prepared you for his arrival, but our talks did not mitigate your reaction. I'm not sure if it was naiveté or blind optimism that allowed me to convince myself that neither you nor I would go through much of an adjustment with his birth. But my work as a child psychologist and my two years of parenting experience did very little in seeing us through this major life change.

Prior to Jake's arrival, you seemed excited about having a new sibling, but that soon changed. It was late at night when I went into labor. You were sound asleep when Dad and I went off to the hospital, leaving Aunt Allie behind to look after you. When you awoke the following morning, you were upset to find us gone. We returned later that evening with the baby in tow. I remember sitting on my bed with Jake in one arm and you to the other side of me. You were so upset that you refused to talk to me. While many children might have softened after a few minutes, you held your ground for the next twenty-four hours. You were stubborn, even at that tender age.

Of course, you came to embrace the idea of our family growing from three to four. Your status had been elevated to *big sister*, and you took that to heart, watching over and protecting your brother. Jake, in turn, adored shadowing you around the house and mimicking your words and actions. Somewhere along the line, you decided that your cousin, Aaron, was a safer target for your jealousy. You argued with him, vied for attention, and saw to it that he took the blame for things that you and Jake had done.

As you and your brother got older, the competition increased, especially when it came to grades. Jake had such an easy time of it all through school. You, on the other hand, found the academic demands much more difficult. Even when you were both older and in college, Jake continued to cruise while you wrestled with coursework. Math and science were particularly frustrating, resulting in you abandoning your dream to become a doctor. How difficult it must have been when your brother seemed to have his pick of careers.

And that is where more regrets come into play for me. I felt terrible that your studies were often so cumbersome. I wanted to make life easier for you. I wanted you to be confident, to have more success as you tackled things. If I had it to do over again, I would have found better alternatives for you—academic environments that were more supportive, more conducive to addressing your learning disability. And I would have pushed you less, not engaged in the nightly struggles around homework. I know that my own frustration often increased the stress you already felt. How I wish that I could take that back and be the kind of mother who was better able to convince you of your talents. Life dealt you some unfair blows. I'm sorry you're not here for me to tell you how proud I am of you.

You didn't live long enough to come to terms with who you were and to truly be able to recognize your strengths. When you died, you were still at a point in life where you were questioning and searching, but your gifts were many. You were the one who was full of energy and always up for the next adventure. You were the dancer, the child full of grace and agility. You were the one who was so full of words and steadfast opinions. I can only imagine where those gifts would have taken you.

*   *   *   *   *

Jake arrives home. As I wrap him in my arms, I think that I will never let him go. I'll stay like this with my wet cheek pressed up against his scruffy beard, our arms tightly wound around each other.

Jake looks tired. His clothes are wrinkled, and his skin is sticky and musty smelling from all the hours on the plane. I offer food, a shower, suggest a nap. As I follow him around the house, I am reminded of him as a toddler following you from room to room. I hang on his every word, grateful that he has come home safe and sound. Even though I have talked with him multiple times each week and seen hundreds of pictures that chronicle his adventures, now that he is home, I want to hear it all again. Jake tolerates the attention, all too aware that he has become the sole focus for my maternal inclinations.

One child has returned home. I can't help but think that I want both of you here with me. It's unfair that you are not permitted the same homecoming as your brother.

* * * * *

Your homecoming is close now
only days away
I count the hours
imagine what it will be like
to hold you, inhale your scent
hear your laughter
and feel my hand in yours

You're almost home
you visit me in my dreams
in my waking hours
you shadow me throughout my day
your essence precedes you
I hold on to your letters and pictures
all traces of you
I await your homecoming
and you
           Reanne, 2004

* * * * *

     Yesterday my brother went away to Outdoor School. It is really weird not having him around because the house is really quiet because I have a very loud brother. I have always wanted to see what it would be like to be an only child but it does get pretty boring. It seems really weird without my little brother always bugging me. It just may be that I don't really want to be an only child even though sometimes he really bugs me sooooooo much that I wish I was. I just would miss my brother just a little if he weren't home.
     Rebecca, February 8, 1994

Becca at 21 with Jake

Forty Seven

Once or twice in a lifetime
A man or woman may choose
A radical leaving, having heard
Lech lecha — Go forth.

God disturbs us toward our destiny
By hard events
And by freedom's now urgent voice
Which explode and confirm who we are.
We don't like leaving,
But God loves becoming.
    Rabbi Norman Hirsh, "Becoming", God Loves Becoming

A celebration of your life...

Your birthday nears; my nights are filled with restless sleep, disturbing dreams, and early morning awakenings. The circles under my eyes darken with the lack of sleep. I try to remember what I did last year to survive the first of your birthdays without you.

The memories refuse to come. Perhaps it doesn't make a

difference. After all, one year has passed and so much has changed. What remains the same is the missing you and wanting you here with me.

Ambivalent as to how to spend your birthday, I make plans and then change them over and over again before accepting a dinner invitation from Aunt Allie. The day before your birthday, I sit in your room and cradle a picture of the two of us. Overcome with sorrow, I call Allie and back out of dinner, telling her that I am too sad to come over.

By morning, I have reconsidered, but the truth is that neither decision brings me any peace. I am sad and agitated through much of the day, flipping back and forth about whether to stay home. Later in the day, Jake finds me in tears. As he holds me, I feel his body tremble against mine as his own grief surfaces. Perhaps we both need to cry.

In the end, we go to Allie's for dinner. Being able to mourn and to remember as a family soothes me a bit.

*   *   *   *   *

Months ago, we decided that the unveiling of your headstone would wait until after Jake's homecoming. Now, five days after your birthday, we are faced with this task. Despite my trepidation, I am determined that the unveiling be a tribute to you and a celebration of your life. Before leaving the house, I rummage through my collection of ocean glass and select a piece to take with me to the cemetery. The edges of the glass are smooth against my fingers as I slip it into my pocket.

Family and friends converge at your grave. The grave and headstone are covered with a white sheet. Conversation stops as we play a recording of Joan Baez singing *Forever Young*. Years ago at your baby naming ceremony, these poetic words summed up our hopes and dreams for you. One year since your passing and the words have been transformed into something that is bittersweet.

The day is unseasonably warm, and the dazzling winter sunshine exaggerates the colors and contours of the cemetery. As the shroud-like sheet is taken up and folded, I stare at the gray headstone and wonder why we didn't think to mark your resting place in brilliant hues of yellow and orange. Wouldn't bright colors have been more in keeping with your personality and the way you lived your life?

Grandma Barbara is one of the first to speak. Through her tears, she tells us how much you would have enjoyed this warm day and suggests that you would have been at the beach. I slide my hand into the pocket of my pants and finger the ocean glass. Grandma's words carry me back to happier times.

She shares how difficult it was to find the right words to say today; nothing she wrote quite met her expectations. She recalls that as the unveiling approached, she heard your words and used them as a guidepost: *"Just tell them the way you and I felt about each other. Tell them about our relationship."*

Grandma has taken your message to heart. "Rebecca was our first grandchild," she begins. "She was full of energy and always in continual motion. Rebecca liked to talk nonstop. When she was a little girl, she loved to sail through the air on the tire swing that Grandpa had suspended from the tree in the backyard. Becca was the oldest and therefore the ringleader of our seven grandchildren. She was radiant, and adventuresome, and was someone who typically wore her emotions on her sleeve."

I smile at the picture she draws of you.

"Becca was a special gift," Grandma continues, "a gift who was taken from us far too soon."

Grandpa Mesh clears his throat and straightens to his full height. I am surprised as he begins to talk, having assumed that he would choose to keep his remembrances to himself. He talks about your love of the ocean and recalls that your happiest moments were at the water's edge.

He is brief and to the point, but his closing words are

poignant and heartfelt. "Rebecca changed our lives," he says. "I miss her."

Your father remembers that you were the one who held others in the family together. He speaks of the lessons he learned from your life and death. Grandma Bern describes you as a toddler taking walks with Grandpa Irwin and hunting for leaves and rocks that you would show us upon your return. Your cousin, Bria, talks about how much you meant to her and the other cousins. The depth of her grief is palpable. She recalls the children in the family looking up to you and shares that she has learned not only from your successes, but from your struggles as well. Inspired by you, she and Tahli have cut their hair and donated it to an organization that makes wigs for children who have lost their own hair to cancer.

As we prepare to recite the *Kaddish*, I clutch the ocean glass in my hand, then set it down on your headstone, between your name and the image of a dragonfly. Seeing your name on the stone makes your death all the more real. A year has gone by but I still hope, still pray for a miracle that this is all some terrible mistake.

Rebecca Amy Singer-Beilin
December 15, 1980—November 27, 2003
In our hearts always...forever young

This seems a fitting tribute along with the Hebrew words: *Lech l'cha* which translate to: *Go forward on your journey.*

Now, we are ready to say the Mourner's *Kaddish*. Voices swell around me, sweeping me along as we recite the familiar words. *"Yitgadal v'yit'kadash sh'mei raba..."*

We end with *L'Chi Lach*, the Debbie Friedman song that was played at your *Bat Mitzvah*. Like so many other things this year, this song takes on new meaning. It no longer speaks to me about my hopes for your life in this world, but rather my hopes for you in the world beyond. Still, it remains a mother's earnest prayer. I sing the words with intention and deliberateness. They are an offering, a wish, all that I can give you from so far away.

> *L'chi lach, to a land that I will show you*
> *Lech l'cha, to a place you do not know*
> *L'chi lach, on your journey I will bless you*
> *And you shall be a blessing*
> *And you shall be a blessing*
> *And you shall be a blessing, l'chi lach*
> *L'chi lach, and I shall make your name great*
> *Lech l'cha, and all shall praise your name*
> *L'chi lach, to the place that I will show you*
>
> *L'sim-chat cha-yim*
> *L'sim-chat cha-yim*
> *L'sim-chat cha-yim l'chi lach*
> > *Debbie Friedman and Savina Teubal,*
> > *Based on Genesis 12:1-2*

* * * * *

Dear Mommy,

I'm writing you a letter which is something I haven't done in such a long time. I'm writing because I want to let you know that I care. I love you <u>so</u> much. I don't always tell you that but I know it is really important so I will say it more often. Mom, I cut my hair as you have noticed. I hope you like it or will eventually like it. I know you like long hair better or at least on me. I really wanted to cut it. I really want you to like it because your opinion of me is really important to me even though I have said at one time or another that I don't care. But I do! At least it will always grow long again. I wanted to let it grow long for you, well also for me, but I guess I wanted it short more. I think you are beautiful anyway you are so I want you to think that about me too. I know you do. Please tell me what you honestly think. Honesty sometimes hurts but it's worth so much more than a lie.

I know I've also been thinking about gratitude and respect and I'm going to try much harder to be more respectful of you. I know that I never hurt anyone more than I have hurt you in the past. Well, that was the past and I will change for the future. You're so important to me and I should treat you like it.

I really should go to sleep because it is rather late. So, remember that I will always love you no matter what changes.

Love, Becky
July 21, 1997

Forty Eight

It is not the length of life, but depth of life.
  Ralph Waldo Emerson, *Collected Works of Ralph Waldo Emerson*

All the memories, all the stories—they flit through my mind like fireflies that skirt about in the darkness...

Compelled to record all the stories so they do not disappear, I make lists in my head, then jot them down on scraps of paper and file them away on a shelf in the den that I have set aside for my writings about you. I view the words like tiny seeds needing to be gathered up and planted. If I don't tend to them, they might dry up and blow away.

I need to be able to tell others about your life. But how to make sense of it all? How to organize these memories that rush in, swooping down when I am trying to work, keeping my mind occupied when I desperately need to sleep? It is easy to get lost in your diary and in the essays you wrote for school.

Save this one, too, I tell myself. *All of it, every morsel. This is what is going to see me through to the next day and the next.*

I have to remember how you were at one year, at two, at

ten. I have to hold on to all of it. There was one night when you were about eighteen months old. We were out to dinner at a Chinese restaurant with Grandma and Grandpa. It had been a busy day and you were worn out. After a few bites of food, you slumped forward and rested your head on the table. You were sound asleep, your hand resting in the plate of food. I haven't thought about that in years. *Better write it down with the others*, I tell myself.

When you were about four, Dad and you went off on errands for an hour or so. On the drive home, Dad pointed out a fire station and used that as an opening to talk with you about all the different things you could be when you were grown—a fire-fighter, a teacher, a dancer, a doctor....

You waited until he had stopped rattling off the list of occupations and then with great seriousness said, "I want to be a duck!"

You weren't trying to be funny or cute, simply thought that being a duck would be a grand aspiration.

More and more stories to gather. One leads to the next and the next. Images that I had set aside are now unearthed; sounds, sights, smells—they all come to life again. When you were five, you cut Jake's hair. While you and Jake played in your room, I tended to chores around the house. I had no idea that you had secured a pair of scissors and in the twenty minutes of being unsupervised had cut not only your hair, but your three-year-old brother's as well. I was shocked when you and Jake appeared in the doorway of the living room to show me your achievement. Your long hair was no more; it was inches shorter, the uneven strokes leaving you looking ragged and unkempt. And your brother...what remained of his hair were close cropped, uneven curls that too had to be reworked to look presentable. Neither you nor your brother were at all upset with the outcome of your effort. I couldn't get too angry with you because you had meant no harm. You were simply being the big sister who was grooming her younger brother.

Besides, it was I who left the scissors within reach; the scenario could have been much worse. There were no flesh wounds, no blood from the experiment. You took my gentle reprimand in stride and nodded in earnest as I explained that scissors were not to be touched without supervision.

That wasn't the only time you showed a particular interest in grooming. Later that same year, you directed your creative talents toward a friend. You and Rachel had spent the afternoon playing together. By the end of the day, the two of you were upstairs in your room. I was in the kitchen making dinner when Rachel's mother arrived to take her home. When I called up to you, the two of you came down the stairs with hair slicked back and glistening. A strong odor emanated from both of you. You reported that you and Rachel had gotten into the bathroom cupboards and drawers where you had made a paste of everything you could find—Ben Gay, toothpaste, antibiotic ointment, shampoo, conditioner, whatever was within reach. You had then smeared the concoction on your heads. You and Rachel explained that you were playing "beauty shop" and were conditioning your hair. It was obvious to me that it had been a cooperative effort with neither one of you as the leader. I saw the whole thing as rather funny, but Sheila was not amused, concluding that Rachel had been the target of your irresponsible efforts. I offered a vague apology for not having supervised better. Sheila hustled Rachel off to the car. I imagined that a shower and multiple shampoos would be their top priority upon arriving home.

Enough memories to hold in the cup of my hand. I think about planting them, watering, feeding them, watching them grow. Long after I, too, am gone from this world, these memories will continue—sturdy plants that progress through their own cycles, producing new buds and blossoms each year, transitioning through a time of rest, of falling away, only to sprout new shoots of life with the changing season. I think about Jake, about his children, and theirs as well. I think about the passing on of a family's history, a family's *rootedness* to one another. You are in that history, Rebecca; your stories will continue on.

The year you turned six, we held your birthday party at the park. You were so overwhelmed by all the attention that you climbed into the car to take a break from friends and family. During that same period, I was intent on baking healthy treats rather than sugar laden desserts. Do you remember the carrot birthday cake with the cream cheese frosting? Sounds all right, doesn't it, until you add in the fact that the main sweeteners were applesauce and dehydrated peaches. None of your friends were thrilled with the fare. Your aunts and cousins still tease me about subsequent years when I would announce that it was time for birthday cake and your friends would either decline or scatter.

You were strong-willed and courageous. After an emergency appendectomy at age thirteen, you refused to miss the ballet performance you had spent months preparing for. So, only a few days after surgery, you donned your tights and leotard, determined that you were going to dance. No amount of cajoling or reasoning would dissuade you. We called Dr. Tom to weigh in on the decision. He advised that we allow you to decide how much you could handle. The entire family came to watch your performance. You carried yourself like a real trooper, despite the exhaustion and pain. At the end of the show your complexion was pale and sallow. We hurried you home where you spent the rest of the day recuperating.

It was that same stubborn determination that helped you succeed as well as you did in school. Despite your frustration about the learning disability, you kept up with your friends and classmates. I rummage through your writings and think, *I have to include this short note you wrote to me. It is too much a part of you to let it disappear.*

1. *Tell the teacher that I am a smart kid and that I am not stupid, but that sometimes I have a hard time.*
2. *Also tell her that I don't want her to make me stand out from other kids in class.*

I refold the slip of paper and slide it into a notebook with your other treasures. *There, it is done,* I think; *that part of Becky is safe and secure. I won't forget. Others won't forget.*

The year you were thirteen, your middle school sponsored a trip to Washington D.C. You had never been so far away from home without Dad or me. You were eager to go on the trip, but once across the country, you became homesick. You called often, seeking reassurance. There were nights when you and your friend, Ariana, slept in the same bed, comforted and more secure in each other's presence. Your class toured the Smithsonian. Breaking into small groups of four or five, you were allowed to roam through the museum on your own for an hour or so. You and another friend, Aliza, became separated from the group. When you were unable to reach me by phone, you placed a tearful phone call to Aunt Allie, who had you scan the area for someone in uniform who might be able to help you.

As a teen, you loved scary movies and ghost stories. Convinced that a house around the corner was haunted, you decided that our house was as well. For a long time, you were uneasy about being home alone. If I happened to be out for the evening, you preferred to have your brother or a friend with you for security.

And then something shifted. You became completely at ease with being on your own, seemingly fearless in fact. It didn't bother you to stay at the house if I was out of town, didn't faze you at eighteen to move to San Diego and live in an apartment with a roommate whom you had just met. You did so much work conquering your childhood fears. What an amazing young woman you had become!

All the memories, all the stories—they flit through my mind like fireflies that skirt about in the darkness. Grab hold of them, capture their light, their energy. That's how I hold on to you and your life.

*   *   *   *   *

Today is Friday, a dance day, but I have been going to dance and watching the class because I can't dance because of my surgery. But you probably think why would I need to watch class? Well, I need to watch class because I just got moved up to a new level. So they don't want me to get behind but also they are starting tryouts for the "Nutcracker" so today I'm going to try class but I'm probably going to have to sit down and rest most of class. I'm really glad I get to Dance Again!!!!!!!!!!!!!!!!!!!

Rebecca, June 10, 1994

Becky at 13

Forty Nine

The gaps are the thing. The gaps are the spirit's one home, the altitudes and latitudes so dazzlingly spare and clean that the spirit can discover itself like a once-blind man unbound...
Annie Dillard, Pilgrim at Tinker Creek

They say that after the loss of a loved one, life goes on...

Time has not made your death any easier for me. The sadness has not lessened; there are not fewer times of missing you. I have not stopped listening for your voice or the sound of your footsteps. I haven't stopped reaching for your hand or craving the feel of your arms around me. People tell me that I am doing better. They want to believe that my heart has stopped aching for you every single moment of every day. They take my increasing calmness as a sign of adjustment and acceptance.

What they fail to understand is that the pain from your death does not let up. It is relentless. The raw, gaping wound inside of me has become an integral part of who I am. It helps to define me. I am the mother of two amazing children, one of this world and one not. I am the mother of a beautiful and sensitive young man who is wise and mature beyond his years.

I am also the mother of a girl who touched me with her smile and her laughter and who demanded my attention with her strong opinions and her temper. I am a woman who carries a hurt so deep and penetrating that it forever changes who I am in this world.

Ironic as it seems, I want to hold on to this hurt. I don't want it to disappear. My pain teaches me to hold fast to life and to cherish my blessings wherever I am fortunate enough to find them. It encourages me to treasure the family and friends I love and to appreciate the fragile and vulnerable qualities of life. It increases my awareness of God and helps me accept that there truly is a purpose to life and to death.

You were always a believer in there being more to us and to our lives than what we could readily perceive. You were so full of questions and opinions. Although you refused to blindly accept the doctrines and teachings of religion, you wanted God to view you as respectful and sincere. You wanted to understand more than your twenty-two years allowed. You questioned and explored, but deep in your soul you were convinced there was a force stronger than us, a force that guided us. I feel that force now more than ever. I am searching. I am trying to learn and to understand. You are a part of my journey. I know that.

I am comforted when I see your fleeting movements, when I hear you and feel you. When these experiences elude me, I turn to my belief in your continuing existence for solace. In the months following your death, I had so many more tangible encounters with you than I do now. These interactions have faded, giving way to more subtle reassurances of your ongoing existence. I prefer the dramatic appearances, but that is beyond my control. It is not my choice when or how I experience you. All I can do is believe and strive to remain open and accessible to these happenings. I am learning patience and faith.

They say that after the loss of a loved one, life goes on.

And so it does, but for me it seems to go on in unexpected ways. My life is full of new dimensions and directions. To many people, I suppose, I am the same person I have always been; but to me, I seem very different. Not unlike a cancer survivor, I have undergone a transformation. I have a deeper appreciation of life. Though it sounds like a cliché, I am aware that life is a gift, one that is far too often cut short. *Cherish it while you have it,* I tell myself. *There are no guarantees, no promises.* I have a greater understanding of my own spirituality and am more linked to my faith and to God. Your death could have eroded these connections; instead it has strengthened them. My fear of death has diminished. Rather than seeing death as the end, I have come to understand that it is simply another phase in our existence. While I do not claim to completely understand what happens after we die, I know that death is not the worst thing that can befall us. It is not something to fear; it is something to accept.

I hold you close, Rebecca. I smile at the sound of your voice and at my remembrances. Long before you ever came into this world, you were my child. I imagined you, anticipated your arrival. You were in my heart and in my dreams. Even after your departure from this world, you remain my girl, my child.

*   *   *   *   *

When I Remember

When I think of you
I don't want it to be with sadness
I want to remember
you were rays of light
strands of music
constant movement
energy

I want to remember
your voice
the arguments
the struggles for independence
I want to remember
how you challenged me
insisting that I grow

I want to remember your laughter
the smile that filled a room
with its stunning radiance
I want to see the ribbon of auburn hair
reaching halfway down your back
the subtle etch of muscles
beneath your sun-bronzed skin

I want to remember the girl
who filled my world with life
I want to remember
the tender soul
the profound love
I want to remember all this, Rebecca,
in thinking of you
        Reanne, December 9, 2004

*   *   *   *   *

I remember a time when I disagreed with my mom because I really wanted to go to this party that I was invited to, but my mom didn't want me to go because she didn't like the people that were going to be there. My mom liked my friend but she didn't like some of the people that would be there. So I ended up not going and being really upset. The next day my friend and I talked at school and she said that I was really lucky I didn't come to the party because she and her mom were spending their whole time getting people to calm down because it had gotten so out of hand. This situation has taught me that I should respect my mom because she knows what she is talking about and wants to protect me.

Rebecca, February 6, 1995

Fifty

You can't rush a prayer to God,
If it comes from the heart
It will rush out on its own
Speed through receding galaxies or
Silences in the soul,
And God will hear.

> Rabbi Norman Hirsh, "Personal Prayer", *Unfolding*
> *Towards Purpose: Reflections, Commentary, and Poems*

I must forgive myself and God as well; I must forgive you...

Walking into the synagogue on Friday night, I am calmer, more settled than I have been in a long time. I welcome the opportunity to pray with community, to sing the ancient melodies, and to chant the Hebrew prayers.

As we move from the *Mi Chamocha* to the petitionary prayer of the *Hashkiveinu,* I consider the meaning of this prayer, the words that ask for God to watch over us and to keep us safe throughout the night. Isn't this also a parent's wish for their child?

In the first days after you died, I was angry at God

because neither God nor I had protected you from a premature and violent death. I had often asked God to watch over you, expected that this was part of the contract. Had God not heard my prayers? Was I not worthy enough to be listened to?

But that anger was tied to the notion of an omnipotent God. What if that is incorrect? What if God is not all-knowing or all-powerful? What if God does not bother to manipulate all the details of our lives, but rather gives us the ability to understand right from wrong and to make choices and weigh consequences? What if God provides each of us with a mind, a heart, and a soul and leaves the rest up to us? If I accept that God is not omnipotent in the sense of monitoring our every move, then I become more able to forgive God for your death. And if I forgive God, then perhaps I can forgive myself as well.

I taught you to make good decisions and to respect the gift of life. I know that you did not want this fate of dying young. You made a bad decision, one with a harsh consequence, but not one of your own choosing.

Hashkiveinu, Adonai Eloheinu. I recite the words with more passion and humility. My prayer does not ensure my safety nor that of my loved ones. We are in partnership with God. Sometimes, in spite of our best efforts, the unthinkable happens. Even still, I do not relinquish my prayers. I continue to hold fast to them; I continue to hope. If I am to preserve my sanity, I must forgive myself and God as well; I must forgive you.

*   *   *   *   *

Reanne Singer

10 Commandments of My Childhood

not to use foul language
be the best I can be
be honest
not to tattle on others
be considerate and respectful of family
treat others the way I want them to treat me
be responsible
take the blame for the things I do
not to take drugs
not to take things that aren't mine
not to be racist
            Rebecca, 1993

Epilogue

I bequeath myself to the dirt to grow from the grass I love,
If you want me again look for me under your boot-soles.

You will hardly know who I am or what I mean,
But I shall be good health to you nevertheless,
And filter and fibre your blood.

Failing to fetch me at first keep encouraged,
Missing me one place search another,
I stop somewhere waiting for you.
Walt Whitman, "Song of Myself", Leaves of Grass

Your substance is a butterfly's whisper that hovers just beyond my
grasp...

Time moves forward, and much has happened in the past year. The sentencing hearing for Tommie provides me with the opportunity to address the Court. I am uneasy about taking on this challenge. Despite this, there is much soul searching, much pain, in deciding what to ask.

On the day of sentencing, I am up early, dressing in

slacks, blouse, and a jacket. I wear your silver dragonfly and heart around my neck. Bob and I drive to the courthouse in silence, both consumed by our own feelings and thoughts.

Once inside, I am keyed up. As Tommie's case is called, I break out in a cold sweat. My senses are heightened as I brace for what is to come. I look away from family and friends to Tommie. He is clad yet again in the same blue shirt and dark slacks he has worn to court before. His image burns into my mind, an unwelcome brand that I will carry away with me.

One breath after the next, slow and steady. Soon it will be my turn to speak. Bob squeezes my hand and then I am on my feet, my written statement before me, the paper shivering in my trembling hands.

You owe this to yourself, to Becca, I think. Another breath. I need for Tommie to hear the heartbreak in my voice. He has to understand how his carelessness has devastated me.

My mouth is dry. I swallow to rid myself of the sour taste. Why didn't I think to bring water or a hard candy? Already, the tears are surfacing. I suck in more air and look down at my typewritten words.

"It's intimidating to try to set down in black and white the immensity of losing my child," I begin, "but that's exactly where I find myself today."

There, I've made it through the first sentence. Move on to the next and the next.

I tell the Court about what it was like to be your mother, about the challenges and all the things I so valued in you. The room is quiet as I talk about you being opinionated and stubborn. I glance over at Tommie, but he's not looking at me, only staring straight ahead. His affect is flat, as though he's keeping himself as far away from my pain as he possibly can.

I lower my gaze back to the words in front of me and continue to read. "Rebecca was beautiful and radiated energy and enthusiasm. Like most children, Becca presented her own set of challenges. It might have been easier to have a docile, soft-spoken child, but there was so much I gained by having Rebecca as my daughter. I wouldn't trade a single moment I had with her."

My father reaches for a tissue and dries his eyes. I hear others in the family sniffling, crying softly. *Keep reading; keep going,* I tell myself. My gaze lifts from the paper. I see the judge watching me, his face somber.

Eyes back down to the paper. "As a parent, I prayed for my child to be safe and healthy," I say, then rattle off the typical childhood illnesses that you survived, the modest injuries that resulted in stitches. I tell them about your appendectomy, share with them the image of you being wheeled down the long hallway to surgery and me holding it together until you were out of sight and then crumbling into tears.

I tell them how excited we all were when you got your first pair of toe shoes for ballet and recount your first solo dance when you floated across the stage.

"I cling to these memories because now that's all that's left me." And then my gaze lands on the next word: *Thanksgiving.* My hands shake harder; my breathing is pressured. I am cold and dizzy. *Calm down. Get through this.*

"Thanksgiving day, 2003, ripped my world apart." *One more word, one more sentence, get through them a piece at a time. Is Tommie listening?* Again, I look his way, but he gives no indication that what I am saying has anything at all to do with him.

I describe that morning when the man came to the door to tell us that you had died. I recite the litany of all that I have lost, all that *you* have lost. I take everyone in the room on a journey through the past year.

"The tragedy of Rebecca's death has impacted all who were close to us," I say. "I have seen the toll it has taken on my parents, my husband, my son, and Rebecca's father. I watch as my nieces and nephews try to function in the world without

Reanne Singer

their oldest cousin. I listen to their words and their moments of silence. They shouldn't have to deal with such grief at such young ages. None of us should. This isn't the direction life was supposed to lead us. This wasn't in the plan. I was going to grow old with both my children nearby. Rebecca used to tell me that when I was old, she would take care of me. She would let me live with her, but it would be by her rules. She'd laugh and tell me that I had set the rules for her as a child. When I reached old age, I'd have to accommodate to her rules. That, too, has been stolen from us.

"I miss my daughter more than I can put into words. I loved Rebecca with my entire heart and soul. I continue to do so. Nothing the Court can put into place will ever take away the hurt that follows me every day."

I look up at the judge for a long moment before continuing on. I tell the Court that I have heard that Tommie continues to drink and drive. What will it take for him to confront his problem with alcohol and do something about it?

The words pour out. I tell the Court that Tommie has never once communicated his condolences to us, never once given any indication that he feels badly for what he has done. I ask the Court to impose a prolonged period of confinement along with mandatory alcohol and drug treatment. I implore the Court to impose a sentence that will reduce the chances of further tragedies happening at Tommie's hand. I make these requests with the hope that Tommie will take the opportunity to change his life.

In the end, I am disappointed when the judge gives Tommie only three years probation and one year in jail. Tommie ends up serving very little time, spending the majority of his term in a work furlough program in which he is allowed to hold down a job in the community and report to a minimum security facility at night. It is more like sleeping at a motel than being incarcerated.

292

Strangely enough, until the sentencing was final, I believed that if I said just the right words in court, if I did a good enough job in representing how your death has affected us, I would be able to bring you home with me once again. I would be able to go back and change everything that has brought us to this moment. With sentencing over, I am confronted yet again with the harsh reality of your death. Nothing eases that. Nothing brings you home to me. I am in the center of a tornado; my emotions spin around me.

We become embroiled in negotiations about a civil suit. Reviewing depositions from those who survived the crash is difficult, but also provides some comfort. The declarations reinforce that you were not a heavy drinker and most likely, had not been drinking the night of the crash. How challenging it must have been for you to be with that group of friends while maintaining your own boundaries and limits. That realization makes me proud.

Throughout the year, I continue to write about you and my journey since your death. As I approach the two year mark, my writing slows; my experiences of you shift. I feel you less often, less dramatically. Your substance is a butterfly's whisper that hovers just beyond my grasp. I know with greater assurance and conviction, that you continue to exist. I look forward to and am soothed by the times when I sense you close at hand. I relish the moments when you hold me and comfort me.

*　　*　　*　　*　　*

Two years later. I am different—sadder, wiser, more at peace with myself than I was before. Your brother has given me a purpose to continue on. In Israel for the first year of his rabbinic studies, Jake has found a direction and a passion. I look forward to him becoming a rabbi. I take pleasure in the simple parts of my existence. A sunset can bring me to tears; rain pattering against the roof can hold my attention for minutes on end.

The devastation and loss that accompanied your death are now part of the fabric of my life. In spite of your death, or perhaps because of it, I have discovered how to live alongside the sorrow. I am finally able to think of you and smile, rather than to always cry. I have accepted that there is growth to be had from grief; I have made the choice to nurture that growth and to be open to it. Even the most trivial and mundane experiences trigger memories of you. My life has become a multicolored cloth that is woven from strands of memory and dreams, from my day-to-day existence in this realm, and from my experiences of you from the Other Side, from the World to Come. My life takes on more depth and dimension as I move forward through this amazing journey.

I miss you and honor you with our memories; I learn how to live without you here. People are right; life goes on. The choice is whether or not I allow myself to be part of it. The answer is clear. I choose life. In my heart, I know that you would approve and offer your blessing.

I think about the wisdom that is out there in the world, the wisdom that has come to me since your passing. Words from loved ones and strangers alike have served as guideposts that help me to navigate the treacherous waters that threatened to cut off my breath when you died. I hold the words in my hands, breathe them in, ingest them, take sustenance from what is offered. I do the same with your words, Rebecca, allow them to show me the way through this terrible grief. And I intermingle my own thoughts and words with those of others until what I have before me is a swirling pool of water that I liken to a *mikvah*. These words have become my ritual bath. I submerge myself in them, am cleansed and sustained by them. This is my way through the grief, my way of living alongside it.

I do not forget nor do I let go. I move forward with intention, with a different perspective than I once had. A mother's love does not stop at the grave. Mine surely hasn't.

*   *   *   *   *

I Am

Make believe friends. A time of innocence,
relaxed and at ease. Oblivious to
the differences that divide. I am
content and comforted. Protected in
parents' arms. Limited understanding
of dangers. Left vulnerable. I am
ambivalent to go back. Wanting more
than memories past. Embracing the child.
A part of me becoming. Now I am.

Rebecca, February 8, 1998

The End

Becca at 22

Acknowledgements

They say it takes a village. So many people were involved in the raising of my two beautiful children. I have also learned that it takes a village to bury a child. I am forever grateful to my family and friends who buoyed me up when I felt like I was drowning in those first months and years after Rebecca's death. Thank you for loving me and for loving Rebecca.

More often than not, it also takes a village to grow a book. *On the Wings of Dragonflies* holds the spirit and voices of so many. My husband, Bob Renard, has been steadfast in his patience, love, and support. He has been sounding board, reality check, strong arms to hold me when I've been overcome by grief, and best friend—always that. My son, Rabbi Jacob Singer-Beilin, has been my reason to keep on living when I was at my lowest. His heart and rabbinic wisdom are a presence in this book. Rabbi Lisa Hochberg-Miller has for years provided spiritual guidance, friendship, and wisdom and has had unfaltering confidence in me writing about my journey. Numbers of friends have provided encouragement. In particular, I want to mention my writers' group friends who have seen me through multiple versions of this book—Ron Kirchoff, Janis Knight, Mary-Jo Murphy, Bob Renard, and Tom

Spisak. Other friends graciously offered input; they include Cheryl Baldwin, Elena DeVos, and Lucianne Ranni. My niece, Tahli Singer-Englar, and my brother-in-law, Bruce Englar, spent hours and hours helping me format the manuscript and cover. My cousin, Julie Singer; my sisters, Leslie and Allison Singer; and my friend, Kate Larsen, kindly proofed the manuscript when I could no longer read it with clarity. I am so grateful to Rabbi David Wolpe who was gracious and kind in providing the foreword to this book.

Surviving the death of my daughter and finding the courage to write about our journey opened the door to conversation and connection where it might not otherwise have happened. I discovered common ground with families who have lost loved ones. I had heartfelt conversations with people here at home and on the other side of the world. I had the privilege of exploring the words of authors, theologians, and philosophers whom I might not otherwise have encountered. I would like to thank the following friends, authors, scholars, and clergy for permission to include their words:

Beyer, Rabbi Elisheva, *Leaving Mitzrayim: A Journey of a Lifetime*, Torah Reading for Week of January 2 – January 8, 2011.

Dickinson, Emily, *"'Hope' Is the Thing with Feathers"* from *The Poems of Emily Dickinson*, edited by Thomas H. Johnson, The Belknap Press of Harvard University Press: Copyright © 1951, 1955, 1979, 1983 by the President and Fellows of Harvard College, Cambridge, Massachusetts.

Dillard, Annie, *For the Time Being*, Knopf: New York, New York, 1999.

—*Pilgrim at Tinker Creek*, Harper's Magazine Press: New York, New York, 1974.

—*Teaching a Stone to Talk: Expeditions and Encounters*, Harper & Row: New York, New York, 1982.

—*The Writing Life*. Harper & Row: New York, New York, 1989.

Englar, Bruce, *Eulogy for Rebecca Singer-Beilin*, 2003.

Friedman, Deborah, with permission from The Deborah Lynn Friedman Trust, *"L'chi Lach"*, text by Debbie Friedman and Savina Teubal, based on Genesis 12:1-2.

Hirsh, Rabbi Norman, *"Becoming"*, *God Loves Becoming*, Published by Rabbi Norman Hirsh: Seattle, Washington, 2005.

—*"Personal Prayer"*, *Unfolding Towards Purpose: Reflections, Commentary, and Poems*, Published by Rabbi Norman Hirsh: Seattle, Washington, 2013.

Horn, Dara, Interviewed by Elizabeth Glixman, E Book Reviews.

Kushner, Rabbi Harold, *When Bad Things Happen to Good People*, Schocken Books: New York, New York, 1978.

Mandell, Sherri, *The Blessing of a Broken Heart*, The Toby Press: New Milford, Connecticut, 2003.

Millay, Edna St. Vincent, *"To a Young Poet"* from *Collected Poems*. Copyright 1939, © 1967 by Edna St. Vincent Millay and Norma Millay Ellis. Reprinted with the permission of The Permissions Company, Inc., on behalf of Holly Peppe, Literary Executor, The Edna St. Vincent Millay Society.

Rapoport, Nessa, "*Undo It, Take It Back*," from *A Woman's Book of Grieving* by Nessa Rapoport. Copyright ©1994 by Nessa Rapoport. All rights reserved.

Rothstein-Fisch, Ariana and Vanessa Moran, "*Introduction to the Kaddish Prayer*", Confirmation, Temple Beth Torah, May 16, 1996.

Singer-Beilin, Rabbi Jacob, *Eulogy for Rebecca Singer-Beilin*, 2003.

Wolpe, Rabbi David, *Making Loss Matter: Creating Meaning in Difficult Times*, Riverhead Books: New York, 1999.

—*Why Be Jewish*: Henry Holt and Company, LLC: New York, New York, 1995.

About the Author

I am fortunate to live in southern California with my husband, my two Australian shepherds, and much of my family nearby. When I'm not writing or working in my clinical psychology practice, I am often painting; gardening; or enjoying time with family and friends. My son makes it out to the West Coast a few times a year, visits that I so cherish.

Writing is my passion. It is a window to my soul, a pathway to the core of who I am and who I want to be. *On the Wings of Dragonflies* is my second published work following *The Storms' Crossing*. I am currently working on a series of adult novels. All of my writing explores what I consider to be the larger questions—morality, faith, courage, identity, and integrity. Elements of my Jewish heritage are woven through much of my work.

On the Wings of Dragonflies is not my book alone. It also belongs to Rebecca. In so many ways, it is a work of love, a book that we created together, a book that mirrors two journeys. I continue to be blessed in having such an incredible daughter.

Also by Reanne Singer:

The Storm's Crossing

Coming soon:

Without A Word
Split Feather

Websites:

reannesinger.weebly.com
wordsabound.weebly.com